Street-Level Bureaucracy in Instructional Design

This book explores the role and function of instructional designers in higher education, highlighting the real-world discrepancy between their actual contributions to organizational growth and the official job descriptions provided by universities.

Investigating how higher education professionals navigate the daily conflict arising from this misalignment, it highlights a number of approaches including improvising to accommodate additional tasks, or strictly adhering job descriptions. The volume is structured around main three themes: the interpretation of instructional design and the role of instructional designers, the concept of street-level bureaucracy and coping strategies, and the contribution of instructional designers to organizational development. The research is grounded in the sociological and management theory of street-level bureaucracy, allowing the author to dissect employee behavior into microelements and connect these to the macro-outcomes of organizational development. The study employs a qualitative approach, using quantitative content analysis and qualitative interviewing on a sample of 17 instructional designers from three different regions in the US. The findings challenge institutional and practice assumptions, offering a new perspective of understanding which asks whether instructional designers are predominantly acting as street-level bureaucrats, or whether behavior and performance is framed by institutional culture and personal characteristics. The author then discusses the implications of these findings for policy, practice, theory, and future research.

It will be of interest to academicians, post-graduate students, and higher education leadership professionals from fields across education, management, instructional design, sociology, and research methods.

Nirupama Akella is an Instructional Designer at Texas A&M International University, US.

Routledge Research in Higher Education

Internships, High-Impact Practices, and Provocative Praxis in Higher Education
A Social Justice Framework Based on Equity, Diversity, Inclusion, and Access
Beth Manke, Bonnie Gasior, and Michelle Chang

Philosophical, Educational and Moral Openings in Doctoral Pursuits and Supervision
Promoting the Values of Wonder, Wander, and Whisper in African Higher Education
Yusef Waghid

Proofreading and Editing in Student and Research Publication Contexts
International Perspectives
Edited by Nigel Harwood

Identity Construction as a Spatiotemporal Phenomenon within Doctoral Students' Intellectual and Academic Identities
Contradictions, Contestations and Convergences
Rudo F. Hwami

An International Approach to Developing Early Career Researchers
A Pipeline to Robust Education Research
Edited by Stephen Gorard and Nadia Siddiqui

For more information about this series, please visit: www.routledge.com/Routledge-Research-in-Higher-Education/book-series/RRHE

Street-Level Bureaucracy in Instructional Design

Perspectives on Professional Identity and Institutional Culture in Higher Education

Nirupama Akella

NEW YORK AND LONDON

First published 2024
by Routledge
605 Third Avenue, New York, NY 10158

and by Routledge
4 Park Square, Milton Park, Abingdon, Oxon, OX14 4RN

Routledge is an imprint of the Taylor & Francis Group, an informa business

© 2024 Nirupama Akella

The right of Nirupama Akella to be identified as author of this work has been asserted in accordance with sections 77 and 78 of the Copyright, Designs and Patents Act 1988.

All rights reserved. No part of this book may be reprinted or reproduced or utilised in any form or by any electronic, mechanical, or other means, now known or hereafter invented, including photocopying and recording, or in any information storage or retrieval system, without permission in writing from the publishers.

Trademark notice: Product or corporate names may be trademarks or registered trademarks, and are used only for identification and explanation without intent to infringe.

ISBN: 9781032713588 (hbk)
ISBN: 9781032731209 (pbk)
ISBN: 9781003426806 (ebk)

DOI: 10.4324/9781003426806

Typeset in Times New Roman
by KnowledgeWorks Global Ltd.

Contents

Preface: A Dream Fulfilled—A Goal Achieved!   x

1 Introduction   1

   Themes and Intentions 2
   Why the Higher Education Sector? 3
   Research Design and Methods 3
   Structure and Style 4

2 Instructional Design: An Overview   7

   History and Evolution of Instructional Design 7
      Instructional Design in Higher Education 8
   Instructional Designer Knowledge and Skill 11
   Instructional Design Themes 13
      Instructional Designer Academic Background vs Experience 13
      Instructional Designer Personal Values 14
      Institutionally Defined Instructional Designer Roles 15
      Influence of Institutional Context and Culture on Instructional Designer Roles 17
         Hierarchical Structures 17
         Flat, Team Structures 18
         Department Cultures 19
      Influence of Availability of Resources on Instructional Designer Roles 20
      Faculty Perceptions of Instructional Designers 21
   Conclusion 22

vi Contents

3 Theory and Design   28

Street-Level Bureaucracy (SLB) *28*
  Macro Dimension *29*
  Micro Dimension *30*
  Institutional/University Narrative *30*
    Institutional Context and Culture *30*
    Finite Resources *31*
    Ambiguous Client Expectations *31*
  Agent/Instructional Designer Narrative *31*
    Professionalism *32*
    Flexible Decision-Making *32*
    Autonomy *32*
    Employee Engagement *32*
  Client/Faculty and Learner Narrative *33*
Research Design/Methodology *33*
  Research Quality *34*
    Credibility *35*
    Dependability *35*
    Confirmability *35*
    Transferability *36*
  My Positionality *36*
    Research Assumptions *37*
    Being Reflexive *38*
  The Research Process *38*
    Research Sites *38*
      River University *39*
      Lane University *39*
      End College *40*
    Sample *40*
      River University *40*
      Lane University *42*
      End College *43*
  Data Collection and Analysis *45*
Conclusion *45*

4 Instructional Designer Perceptions vs Official Job Descriptions   49

River University *49*
  Roles and Functions *50*

  Relation-Building Functions 50
  Support Functions 52
  New Roles 53
 Lane University 54
  Roles and Functions 55
   Support Roles 55
   Responsive Role 57
 End College 59
  Roles and Functions 60
   Project Management 60
   Course Design 61
   Educational Technology 62
   Training 62
   Faculty and Student Liaison 63
   Informal Leadership 64
 Analysis and Conclusion 65
  Job Roles and Functions 66

5 Street-Level Bureaucrats 70

 River University 70
  Department Structure 70
  Culture of Autonomy 71
  Meeting Client Needs 72
  Finite Resources 73
  Personal Characteristics 74
  Discrete Flexibility/Flexible Decision-Making 74
  Professional Development 75
   Coping Strategies 76
 Lane University 77
  Institutional and Department Structure 77
  Department Culture 78
   Being Boxed In 79
   One-Way Communication 79
  Meeting Client Needs 80
  Finite Resources 81
  Personal Characteristics 82
  Autonomy/Flexible Decision-Making 83
  Professional Development 83

End College 85
   A Team Structure and Culture 85
      Functional Fluidity 86
      Team Culture 87
      Meeting Client Needs 88
      Finite Resources 88
      Personal Characteristics 89
      Flexible Discretion 90
      Professional Development 91
      Coping Strategies 92
   Analysis and Conclusion 93

6 Organizational Contribution   98

River University 98
Lane University 99
End College 100
Analysis and Conclusion 101

7 Conclusion and Implications   104

The BIG Conclusion 104
   Instructional Designer Job Behavior Is Influenced by
      Institutional Culture 104
   Instructional Designer Job Behavior Is Influenced by
      Personal Characteristics 106
Implications 107
   Implications for Practice and Policy 107
      Developing a Formal University Definition of
         Instructional Design 107
      Developing Awareness about Instructional
         Design 107
      Dismantling or Changing Dysfunctional
         Cultures 108
      A Conscious Move to Develop Hybrid System 108
      Investing in Professional Development
         Continually 109

Theoretical Implications 109
   Critiquing the Street-Level Bureaucracy Theory 109
   Examining Instructional Designer Job Behavior and
     Performance through the Lens of Organizational
     Culture Theory 110
   Implications for Future Research 111

Wrapping Up 112

Appendix A: Interview Protocol and Questions   *116*
Index   *118*

Preface
A Dream Fulfilled—A Goal Achieved!

This book is an adaptation of my doctoral thesis completed in May 2022 from Wichita State University, Kansas. When I started my doctorate, I was confident and perhaps a bit arrogant—after all I was a professional instructional designer coming from a family of doctoral holders! My doctoral topic was instructional design, and I had already decided on my theory and methodology. I was all set!

But the three years I was a doctoral student and then a doctoral candidate changed me. What I initially wrote as my thesis idea during my first year was not what I actually ended up writing as my thesis in my final year. My topic remained instructional design but the theory, focus, research design, and research methods changed so many times—more than I can remember! I read, searched, read, wrote, re-wrote, complained, cried, shouted, screamed, and even announced my intention to drop out from the program! But I remained and stuck to the program—grumbling, angry—but determined to do what I had started! It took three long, tough, grueling years of research, writing outlines, drafts, presentations, and chapters and listening to my professors that "I was getting there but still had work to do."

And so, I worked, wrote, edited entire chapters, and finally, at the end of my second year, hit upon my actual topic, theory, and appropriate research methodology. That was, indeed, a proud moment of celebration. It gave me the much-needed fuel for the fire to read, research, write, edit, re-write my thesis! And my diligence and hard work paid off! After three tumultuous years resembling an obstacle course, I got my prize—my education doctorate degree! But my journey was not finished!

I wanted to see my hard work; my dream published into a book. And so began another journey—though shorter and much calmer! And now I am adapting my thesis into a book for publication, and I am ecstatic—proud of my achievement!

Of course, I must thank a few very important people without whom I could never, ever have fulfilled my dream and achieved my goal. First in line is my doctoral committee chair, Dr. Jean Patterson. Dr. Patterson—I was lucky to have you as my chair—blessed to have you as my critic, guide, and taskmaster.

I would still be writing and crying if it weren't for you! Now adapting my thesis in a book format has made me appreciate you more!

My committee members deserve my thanks—Dr. Kristin Sherwood, Dr. Victoria Sherif, Dr. Valerie Thompson, and Dr. JaeHwan Byn. All of you helped me think and write better.

Thank you to my contacts and my participants.

And a big thank you to my family! My parents—Ma and Dad, thank you, for supporting me, being my cheerleaders, and telling me that I could do it… my sister, brother, and niece—a big hug and smile!

1 Introduction

Recent events such as the pandemic and the subsequent increase in online and hybrid instruction have transformed, diversified, and expanded the higher education landscape, online and distance learning dynamics, and learner populations. Course and/or instructional design and professionals have suddenly been propelled into the limelight as increasing attention has become focused on the work and identity of instructional designers. Always recognized as core support staff, instructional designers suddenly find themselves in the spotlight with queries about their work process, function, and role in higher education. *Who are instructional designers? What do instructional designers do daily on the job and how do they do it?*

Instructional designers have design and technology expertise with skills of instructional writing, formatting, multi-media, and eLearning which contribute to student learning, success, research, and teaching initiatives (Lowell & Ashby, 2018; Morrison et al., 2019; Moskal, 2012). Their skills also comprise problem-solving, mentoring, and collaborating with faculty, staff, and learners to develop authentic and relevant curricula aligned with their needs and motivations (Halupa, 2019; Iqdami & Branch, 2016; Koszalka et al., 2013; Miller & Stein, 2016; Moskal, 2012). It is not surprising that instructional designers are described as "*jack of all trades*" (Intentional Futures, 2016, p. 10).

Ideal and typical tasks for instructional designers comprise (a) designing effective courses by writing and formatting content into instruction, (b) evaluating new educational technology and eLearning apps, (c) creating, embedding, and implementing multi-media content (i.e., podcasts, videos, and games), and (d) developing, modifying, and improving established teaching and learning models (Halupa, 2019; Richardson et al., 2019). They are also responsible for course and process evaluations, implementing feedback of courses and learning designs, training faculty and other campus personnel about instructional design systems, and researching innovations in instructional technology, instructional design, learning, and education models. Subsequently, instructional design contributions include designing effective, learner, and technologically oriented courses, improving and developing new learning design systems to attract and retain students. Other instructional

DOI: 10.4324/9781003426806-1

designer contributions can comprise faculty professional development by training, mentoring, collaborating with faculty about feasible and suitable methods of curriculum development and delivery. Instructional designers, therefore, should not be regarded only as course designers. They can initiate, plan, and foster innovative learning and instructional technology designs.

However, universities and colleges identify instructional designers as course design help and instructional technology staff who perform tasks of proofreading, editing, and learning management system (LMS) troubleshooting (Magruder et al., 2019; Reiser & Dempsey, 2012; Ren, 2019; Sims & Koszalka, 2008). Consequently, university outlined instructional designer functions do not always align with typical instructional designer functions, thus creating a gap between official job descriptions and functions which instructional designers are capable of and prefer to perform (Acevedo & Roque, 2019; Mitchell et al., 2017; Ren, 2019). This gap between institutional policy and instructional designer practice leads to instructional designers experiencing *dissonance and conflict between what they are capable of and want to do and what they are permitted to do.*

So, what do instructional designers do to be flexible and perform responsibilities and tasks not listed in their official job descriptions? Instructional designers "*have responsibility for making unique and fully appropriate responses to individual clients and their situations*" (Lipsky, 1980, p. 161). Do they work around institutional policy and develop *flexible rules of thumb* to achieve goals of designing learner-oriented instruction and streamlining design processes? Do instructional designers behave as street-level bureaucrats to deal with the daily dilemma, or do they rigidly follow their official job descriptions and ignore the everyday conflict?

In this chapter, I lay the foundation of the book and present the (a) themes/research questions and intentions, (b) research focus, (c) research design and method, and (d) overall structure of the book.

Themes and Intentions

In this book, I explore the gap between practice and policy of instructional designers in higher education. I research instructional designer perceptions about their work, their roles, their functions, and their identity. Who are instructional designers? What do they do? And how do they do it? These three themes are broken into applicable research questions that guide and direct my research.

1 How do instructional designers working in higher education institutions view and define instructional design, their roles, and daily functions as compared to official job descriptions?
2 How do instructional designers exercise street-level divergence?
3 How do instructional designers contribute toward organizational development?

Researching this gap between policy and practice provides university administrators factual evidence for evaluating university job descriptions and actual instructional designer job functions and identifying whether university job requirements align with what instructional designers are capable of doing and prefer to do. This knowledge and understanding would bring about a multitude of much-needed changes in higher education, specifically in terms of utilizing the varied skillset of instructional designers. It would result in the overhaul of official instructional designer job descriptions and accommodate instructional designers' educational technological, learning design, and faculty collaboration expertise instead of focusing on a single skillset. Further, researching this gap would also benefit student learning, faculty professional development, teaching, institutional development, and further the discipline (Harrison & DeVries, 2019; Intentional Futures, 2016; Lowell & Ashby, 2018; Miller & Stein, 2016). Effective, tech-savvy courses aligned with faculty and learner motivations not only increase student learning and success but also promote student enrollment, retention, and university reputation in community as learner-oriented.

Why the Higher Education Sector?

Though found in all sectors ranging from military and manufacturing, banking and healthcare, instructional design is concentrated in the higher education sector (Larson & Lockee, 2004; Morrison et al., 2019; Reiser & Dempsey, 2012). During my literature search on instructional design, I realized that higher education and instructional design share a common purpose and mission. Both higher education and instructional design are founded on constructivist principles of learning and advocate for the design of effective and efficient learner-oriented courses. Higher education institutions and organizations strive for overall education of all diverse learners through effective and technologically savvy courses. While instructional design is the design and development of effective and efficient courses for knowledge and skill transfer from classroom to workspace, as such, instructional design in higher education is a process and science with concise functions and responsibilities to enable and ensure design, development, and delivery of learner-centric technological environments. Hence practitioners of instructional design are scientists who develop educational foundations of every discipline and contribute heavily to molding and shaping future work behavior, thought, and action.

Research Design and Methods

It is not possible to develop and generate a completely impartial detached account of any event occurring in a society and/or world external to us. Individuals always have a personal interest and/or investment in an external event (Habermas, 2015). And this personal interest has the power to color our research interpretations and findings. Likewise, it was difficult for me as a doctoral researcher to view and study the research problem of instructional designers dispassionately. My academic and professional background of a master's degree in Instructional Design and ten years of experience in higher education as an instructional designer and technologist colored my entire research study. I had deep understanding, appreciation, and bias about instructional designers and yet had to strive and maintain an objective outlook. I chose a basic qualitative design with twin diverse methods of quantitative content documentation and analysis and qualitative in-depth interviewing. Qualitative research is individualized and unique where the researcher is a data collection tool. The researcher's educational background, professional experience, beliefs, and perspectives influence the study at all stages starting with choice of research topic, literature review content, data collection, sampling, and interpretation (Creswell & Creswell, 2018; Lapan et al., 2012). Despite my inherent assumptions about instructional designers functioning as street-level bureaucrats in higher educational institutions, the basic qualitative design allowed methodological fluidity and flexibility which enabled me to explore multiple perspectives or *"the dilemmas street-level workers encountered in their work, the way they dealt with these dilemmas; and the motives for dealing with the dilemmas"* (Bachman et al., 2017, p. 137). The design with its diverse methods enabled objectivity in the form of official university job descriptions and at the same allowed subjective construction of instructional designer perspectives through in-depth semi-structured interviewing. The fusion of the quantitative and qualitative methods enabled a data-driven approach where factual information, i.e., job description relevant content, was evaluated and analyzed with instructional designer subjective perspectives in their own words to answer the research questions and purpose. To that end, the basic qualitative design proved an apt fit for this complex and fluid research study.

Structure and Style

The book is formatted like a research monologue and is based on my empirical qualitative doctoral research. As such, despite having a formal structure, I use an informal conversational style of writing in first person as per the current guidelines of APA 7th edition. I have authored the book in a mixture of tenses highlighting an on-going process of thinking and writing: (a) events that are occurring as seen in this introductory chapter and chapter abstracts of all the book chapters and (b) events that have already occurred in the past, i.e., chapter contents which explore facets of the empirical study done.

I have structured my book like the funnel of the research process (Creswell & Creswell, 2018). It lays the foundation and then builds on it with appropriate literature, data, and interpretations. Congruently, this chapter is the foundation of the book. It describes the research problem, research aims and themes, research purpose, and provides an insight into the research design and methods used. Chapter 2 details relevant literature on instructional design discussing meaning, evolution, and various facets of instructional design and subsequently provides an understanding of the research concept. Chapter 3 describes in vivid detail (a) theory used to frame and anchor the research study, (b) the research design, and (c) the research process which comprises research methods, research sample and participants, data collection, and analysis. It also discusses the study's research quality highlighting my positionality which played an important influential role in my study. Chapters 4–6 answer each of the three themes being explored in this study and include an in-depth analysis and conclusion. Chapter 4 answers the first research theme of instructional design meaning, roles, and function. The chapter, interspersed with relevant document and interview excerpts, exudes a data-driven approach consistent with the research design rationale. Chapters 5 and 6, likewise, adopt similar approaches and discuss the second theme of street-level bureaucracy and street-level divergence. Chapter 7 discusses the primary conclusions, policy, practice, theoretical, and future implications. The chapter wraps up with a summative conclusion.

References

Acevedo, M. M., & Roque, G. (2019). Resisting the deprofessionalization of instructional design. In Y. Vovides & L. R. Lemus (Eds.), *Optimizing instructional design methods in higher education* (pp. 9–26). IGI Global. https://doi.org/10.4018/978-1-5225-4975-8.ch002

Bachman, S. S., Wachman, M., Manning, L., Cohen, A. M., Seifert, R. W., Jones, D. K., Fitzgerald, T., Nuzum, R., & Riley, P. (2017). Social work's role in Medicaid reform: A qualitative study. *American Journal of Public Health, 107*(S3), S250–S255. https://doi.org/10.2105/AJPH.2017.304002

Creswell, J. W., & Creswell, J. D. (2018). *Research design: Qualitative, quantitative, and mixed methods approaches* (5th ed.). SAGE Publications, Inc.

Habermas, J. (2015). *Knowledge and human interests*. John Wiley & Sons.

Halupa, C. (2019). Differentiation of roles: Instructional designers and faculty in the creation of online courses. *International Journal of Higher Education, 8*(1), 55–68. https://doi.org/10.5430/ijhe.v8n1p55

Harrison, M., & DeVries, I. (2019). Open educational practices advocacy: The instructional designer experience. *Canadian Journal of Learning and Technology, 45*(3), n3. https://doi.org/10.21432/cjlt27881

Intentional Futures. (2016). *Instructional design in higher education: A report on the role, workflow, and experience of instructional designers*. https://uploads-ssl.webflow.com/61bb092a5c21437cb3a10798/624241a510e63d6f7eee6cd0_Instructional-Design-in-Higher-Education-Report.pdf

Iqdami, M. N., & Branch, R. M. (2016). Examining multimedia competencies for educational technologists in higher education. *TechTrends, 60*(4), 365–373. https://doi.org/10.1007/s11528-016-0064-1

Koszalka, T. A., RussEft, D. F., & Reiser, R. (2013). *Instructional designer competencies: The standards* (4th ed.). IAP.

Lapan, S. D., Quartaroli, M. T., & Riemer, F. J. (2012). *Qualitative research: An introduction to methods and designs*. Jossey-Bass.

Larson, M. B., & Lockee, B. B. (2004). Instructional design practice: Career environments, job roles, and a climate of change. *Performance Improvement Quarterly, 17*(1), 22–40. https://doi.org/10.1111/j.1937-8327.2004.tb00300.x

Lipsky, M. (1980). *Street-level bureaucracy: Dilemmas of the individual in public services*. Russel Sage Foundation.

Lowell, V. L., & Ashby, I. V. (2018). Supporting the development of collaboration and feedback skills in instructional designers. *Journal of Computing in Higher Education, 30*(1), 72–92. https://doi.org/10.1007/s12528-018-9170-8

Magruder, O., Arnold, D. A., Moore, S., & Edwards, M. (2019). What is an ID? A survey study. *Online Learning, 23*(3), 137–160. https://doi.org/10.24059/olj.v23i3.1546

Miller, S., & Stein, G. (2016). Finding our voice: Instructional designers in higher education. *Educause, 10*. https://er.educause.edu/articles/2016/2/finding-our-voice-instructional-designers-in-higher-education

Mitchell, K., Simpson, C., & Adachi, C. (2017). *What's in a name: The ambiguity and complexity of technology enhanced learning roles* [Conference presentation]. Facilitating social learning through learning design: A perspective of collaborative academic development. https://2017conference.ascilite.org/program/,

Morrison, G. R., Ross, S. M., Kemp, J. E., & Kalman, H. K. (2019). *Designing effective instruction* (6th ed.). John Wiley & Sons.

Moskal, T. M. (2012). *Instructional designers in higher education* [Doctoral Dissertation, University of Nebraska-Lincoln]. http://digitalcommons.unl.edu/cehsedaddiss/121

Reiser, R. A., & Dempsey, J. V. (2012). *Trends and issues in instructional design and technology* (R. A. Reiser & J. V. Dempsey, Eds.; 3rd ed.). Pearson.

Ren, X. (2019). The undefined figure: Instructional designers in the open educational resource (OER) movement in higher education. *Education and Information Technologies, 24*(6), 3483–3500. https://doi.org/10.1007/s10639-019-09940-0.

Richardson, J. C., Ashby, I., Alshammari, A. N., Cheng, Z., Johnson, B. S., Krause, T. S., Lee, D., Randolph, A. E., & Wang, H. (2019). Faculty and instructional designers on building successful collaborative relationships. *Educational Technology Research and Development, 67*(4), 855–880. https://doi.org/10.1007/s11423-018-9636-4

Sims, R. C., & Koszalka, T. A. (2008). Competencies for the new-age instructional designer. In M. D. M. J. Michael Spector, J. van Merrienboer, & M. P. Driscoll (Eds.), *Handbook of research on educational communications and technology* (3rd ed., pp. 569–575). Lawrence Erlbaum.

2 Instructional Design
An Overview

There are many definitions of instructional design which are not unified and comprehensive but highlight a specific skill or function. This section presents a few definitions. Instructional design in higher education is identified as a science, a discipline, a process, and a technology (Morrison et al., 2019; Reiser & Dempsey, 2012). It combines educational theory, design principles, instructional technology (IT), and learning science elements. Commonly used in education to design learning content and training, instructional design is used to identify and close performance and productivity gaps. As such, instructional designers are described as architects and engineers of quality learning solutions and experiences (Beirne & Romanoski, 2018; Dick et al., 2005; Koszalka et al., 2013; Morrison et al., 2019). They create effective, relevant, and engaging learning experiences for long-term learning which is transferable to varied workplaces. To do this, instructional designers draw on best practices from education, design, psychology, systems theory, and creative writing to develop eLearning, face-to-face workshops, job aids, and other performance solutions.

In other definitions, instructional design is considered a system that translates neurocognitive principles into learning plans and strategies to develop instructional materials, assessments, and information resources (Acevedo & Roque, 2019; Gustafson & Branch, 2002; Morgan, 2019; Reiser & Dempsey, 2012; Smith & Ragan, 2004). It is also defined as educational and/or IT where technology is used to transform subject-matter into effective instruction to enable deep effective learning (Reigeluth et al., 2008). Instructional designers, therefore, are identified as content developers and instructional/educational technologists who interact with faculty, students, and staff to provide course learning solutions and figure out what processes, tools, and methods to use at what stage (Morgan, 2019; Reiser, 2001b; Ren, 2019).

History and Evolution of Instructional Design

Instructional design originated as a short-term training program to instruct and train soldiers in new methods of combat during World War II (Moskal, 2012; Smith & Ragan, 2004). Psychologists and educators, such as Robert

Gagne, were recruited by the military to develop programmed instructional and training materials. However, post-World War II the scope and focus of instructional design changed from a short-term training design activity in the military to designing and developing instruction for effective learning and problem-solving in the education field.

B. F. Skinner, the American psychologist, in 1954 established a system of practice and reinforcement to develop a programmed, step-by-step model of learning later popularized as the ADDIE model of instructional design (Moskal, 2012). According to ADDIE, developing instruction for learning occurred in systematic sequential steps of (a) analyzing the material, (b) developing the material, (c) designing the material, (d) implementing instruction, and (e) evaluating instruction (Hansen, 2010; Reiser & Dempsey, 2012; Seels & Glasgow, 1998).

Educational psychologists Bloom and Gagne revolutionized instructional design describing it to be an iterative learner-oriented process of designing instruction (Dick, 1996; Hardré, 2005; Moskal, 2012; Seels & Richey, 2012; Smith & Ragan, 2004). Publication of Bloom's *Taxonomy of Educational Objectives* in 1956 followed by Gagne's text, *Conditions of Learning*, in 1965 changed how instruction was developed. Focus centered on helping, ensuring that learners understood, analyzed, synthesized, and applied instructional material to the workplace. Gagne categorized human learning outcomes into five domains: (a) verbal information, (b) intellectual skills, (c) psychomotor skills, (d) attitudes, and (e) cognitive strategies, which further narrowed the field into designing learning for behavioral and performance outcomes. Bloom differentiated between design and teaching and said that design was a framing element separate from teaching modalities. Design was a deliberate, social, and collaborative process where instructional designers had authority and awareness to execute systems and designs beneficial for learning and teaching.

Instructional Design in Higher Education

In the 1970s the broad focus of instructional design as a curriculum design activity in education and military narrowed to a concentrated holistic process of designing instruction for deep learning in higher education using different formats, technologies, and pedagogies (Dick et al., 2005; Dijkstra, 2001; Gustafson & Branch, 2002; Perez & Emery, 1995; Reigeluth et al., 2008). The aim of instructional design changed from short-term learning and performance benefits to long-term learning, understanding, and internalization of classroom content. This internalization would lead to transfer of classroom learning in the workplace and to continual problem-solving and critical thinking. The theory of instructional design was no longer unified but comprised different theories ranging from socio-cognitive theories of development, human learning, systems theory, and human resource development. Instructional design was identified as a goal-based

Instructional Design 9

and learner-oriented linear process of analyzing and assessing learner needs and demands to develop appropriate instruction for optimal performance and productivity (Morrison et al., 2019; Reiser & Dempsey, 2012; Russ-Eft et al., 2013; Smith & Ragan, 2004).

Instructional design underwent a further change in the 1980s and 1990s when the Internet, IT, and digitization swept the educational landscape (Gustafson & Branch, 2002; Moskal, 2012). The manner of designing instruction for traditional learners in brick-and-mortar classrooms changed to fluid online learning formats. Instructional design was re-defined as a human performance technology (HPT) activity that utilized multi-media and web/computer technology to design superior instruction for optimal human performance, organizational growth, and efficiency. Instructional designers, therefore, were responsible for using engaging, relevant, and effective educational/IT in instructional modules to develop job skills, emotional intelligence, and civility (Halupa, 2019). Their function was developing assessments and challenging tasks to enable problem-solving.

In 1995, Shrock re-defined instructional design as a broad umbrella for fluid design activity. It was defined as a *"purposeful activity that results in a combination of strategies, activities, and resources to facilitate learning"* (Sims & Koszalka, 2008, p. 570). The definition tried to be inclusive of all the diverse elements of instructional design. It tried to combine the learning, strategic, contextual, and design elements of instructional design process and formulate a working definition for practitioners. But the definition confused matters more. Scholars and practitioners in higher education struggled to identify instructional design elements, strategies, and resources. Another popular definition which tried to clarify matters described instructional design as a systemic design activity whose goal was to align instructional curricula to organizational values and vision – *"design, development, utilization, management, and evaluation of processes and resources for learning"* (Reiser, 2001a, p. 1; Shearer, 2003). In 2014, the eLearning Guild, a national organization of eLearning, instructional technologists, and instructional designers, stated that instructional design was a learning design activity characterized by adaptiveness, application, skills transference, and problem-solving. Instructional designers were tasked with varying diverse functions such as designing adaptive learning frameworks aligned with organizational policies and context (Hansen, 2010). Other functions were those of coaching and working with faculty to develop instruction for knowledge and skill transference to the workplace. To do this, instructional designers used IT to write and embed challenging problems and tasks. In a nutshell, instructional design was a combination of:

> *many things, and most often it is what you want and need it to be ... This ID [instructional design] thing is no one thing. Some see ISD [instructional systems design] as procedural, algorithmic, characterized by one box*

> each for analysis, design, development, implementation and evaluation, with arrows linking the boxes and dependable steps directing what to do and in what order. They cling to the certainty. Many disagree. They emphasize what goes on inside the boxes, inclining towards a more heuristic approach, with rules of thumb applied in context.
>
> (Munzenmaier, 2014, p. 1)

That is, instructional design attempts to encompass everything and mold itself to every activity and field. However, this chameleon quality of instructional design makes it difficult to provide a singular comprehensive definition.

In 2017, instructional design was again re-defined as a strategic process of social agency where instructional designers were responsible for curriculum design, technology integration, faculty collaboration, and adapting the organization to changing conditions (Acevedo & Roque, 2019; Annand & Jensen, 2017; Morgan, 2019; Vovides & Lemus, 2019). Instructional design was envisioned to be a scholar-practitioner discipline aimed at intentional change aligned to economic, cultural, and social conditions. It was to be an integral organizational process of initiating, empowering, supporting, and transforming organizations to adapt to changing conditions. It was a "*bridge*" activity grounded in research, practice, and dialogue that connected internal organizational functions to external changes (Short & Shindell, 2009, p. 478). Functions of instructional designers, thus, were manifold and diverse. They included faculty and staff collaboration and mentoring to streamlining learning design processes, developing learning management system (LMS) procedures for course integration. Other functions were developing open workplace cultures of flexible, two-way communication channels, transparent accountability, and civility practices (Campbell et al., 2009). Instructional designers networked with staff and executive leaders to bring about policy changes in recruitment, course design, and LMS formats.

However, the onset of COVID has once again re-defined instructional design in higher education as a strategic performance improvement learning design activity (Cowan, 2020; Edmondson, 2020; Fernandez & Shaw, 2020; Xie et al., 2021; Pilbeam, 2021). COVID has impacted how education institutions, learning formats, and delivery systems are organized. Renewed emphasis on digital learning has pushed instructional designers to the forefront of organizing, leading, designing fully online instructional modules. Subsequently, instructional design has become synonymous with IT. Instructional design functions of analyzing learner needs for designing, developing, and evaluating face-to-face instruction have shifted to a mobile online format. This means analyzing learning needs on online learning platforms to find out what courses and forms of learning were preferred by learners on LMS formats (Fox et al., 2020). Instructional designers developed, designed, implemented, and evaluated courses embedded with appropriate IT such as avatars, game based, and virtual 3D learning software to reach diverse learning populations. They collaborated, communicated, and worked in teams as strategic partners with faculty to develop digitally enhanced badge and audit courses such as interactive trainings, synchronous discussion boards, quizzes, and capstone assignments.

Instructional designers designed courses on mobile and social learning apps and networks such as android, iPhones, Facebook, and Twitter for nontraditional online learners who did not have time to invest in traditional LMS learning. Instructional designers were responsible for training executive leadership, staff, and faculty about online content writing and American Disabilities Act (ADA) guidelines (Ali, 2020). In other functions, they collaborated, mentored, coached, networked, and advised leadership and staff to avoid system duplication, merge course design and technology systems to streamline, and align the institution with current state and federal curricula design standards. However, the widespread usage and popularity of artificial intelligence (AI) software and practices of ChatGPT, Time Hero, and Bard have changed the role and function of the instructional designer. AI algorithms, chatbots, and virtual assistants are developing new forms of personalized effective learning engagement pathways (Namatherdhala et al., 2022). These adaptive and intelligent tutoring and learning pathways are developing interactive instruction and creating an instructional environment where instructional designers must share their learning and curriculum designer role with an adaptive immersive AI medium. Jobs and functions of instructional designers are narrowing, and in some cases, as observed in a study by IBM researchers, freeing instructional designers as sole curriculum and learning experience designers to multi-faceted roles of strategic holistic interactive learning experience designers. Their participation in strategic vision and mission development, policy analysis, teaching evaluations, recruitment, and fiscal management has expanded and become integral to higher education. Contemporary instructional designers work with AI software to create focused individualized learning formats that debunk the norm of generalized instruction and "*one size fits all*" approach. They act as learning and/or curriculum design consultants, product, and project managers who are involved with content curation, streamline resources for improved efficiency, productivity, and enhance smooth dialogue and expectations between internal and external higher education stakeholders. AI enables instructional designers to communicate, collaborate with faculty to analyze learner data, predict individual learning graphs, and develop personalized learning and game-based learning experiences.

Instructional Designer Knowledge and Skill

Instructional designer knowledge and skills are identified as competencies or expert ability to develop, design, and implement quality learning solutions for continuous proactive learning and problem-solving (Halupa, 2019;

International Board of Standards, Performance, Training, and Instruction [IBSTPI], 2000; Perez & Emery, 1995; Richey et al., 2001; Russ-Eft et al., 2013; Sims & Koszalka, 2008). Instructional design competencies were initially developed and published by the premier global accrediting organization of instructional design, the *International Board of Standards, Performance, Training, and Instruction (IBSTPI)* in 1983. Updated in 2019, there are currently six competencies: professional knowledge, design and development, planning and analysis, evaluation and implementation, leadership, and management. Professional knowledge is a foundational competency which includes basic knowledge of learning, instructional design, and IT theories and models. Instructional designers, irrespective of their role, function, and rank have this foundational knowledge (Reiser, 2001a; Richey et al., 2001). The other five competencies are developed from this competency. For example, the competency of design and development includes specialized knowledge of learning and instructional design theories with skills of learner needs analysis, selection of instructional strategies and technologies, curriculum development, writing learner and performance objectives, and evaluation of the design project (Richey et al., 2001). Similarly, the competency of planning and analysis includes design and development knowledge and skills to plan, analyze, supervise curricula projects, and distribute resources of budget and technology for course design activities.

Likewise, the competencies of evaluation and implementation, leadership, and management have overlapping knowledge and skills such as writing, project management, communication, collaboration, and team; relationship building. Common knowledge base includes knowledge of learning and instructional design theory, IT hardware, software applications, and LMS. Instructional design competencies emerged as fluid, ambiguous, and ill-defined proving a disservice to the profession and practice of instructional design. Roles of instructional designers became confused and messy as one role merged into another (Halupa, 2019; Intentional Futures, 2016). Instructional designers are learning design experts who have skills of course in writing, analyzing learner needs, collaborating, and communicating with faculty to plan, organize, and develop weekly course content (Gray et al., 2015; Intentional Futures, 2016; Magruder et al., 2019; Moskal, 2012; Oliver, 2002; Richardson et al., 2019). They are described as curriculum leaders who are co-participants in designing, developing, and delivering learner-oriented curricula (Drysdale, 2018). At the same time instructional designers are also IT experts with skills in research, IT, design, multi-media skills, and LMS writing support (Cox & Osguthorpe, 2003; Intentional Futures, 2016; Miller & Stein, 2016; Park & Luo, 2017). Instructional designers, therefore, are supposed to be experts in all competencies and perform all functions. Indeed, it is not surprising that they are identified as "*jack of all trades*" (Intentional Futures, 2016, p. 10).

Narrow description of instructional designer job roles of course design and IT help does not utilize instructional design expertise ranging from learning design leadership, project management, and change agents (Koszalka et al., 2013). In their study, Mitchell et al. (2017) argued that having many competencies gave institutions license to change, distorting the original meaning and function of instructional design for developing effective and efficient instruction. This resulted in a lack of understanding, and poor utilization of instructional design expertise. In another study, Richardson et al. (2019) observed that presence of too many competencies devalued the role of the instructional designer and created situations where university personnel and students did not know who instructional designers were, and what they did every day on the job.

The reason for this ambiguity and confusion is the growing field of instructional design. To quote, *"The field of instructional design has grown in breadth, depth, and complexity such that no one person can be expected to be fully competent in all related skills and knowledge"* (Koszalka et al., 2013, p. 23). Instructional design began as a design activity for developing short-term training and has kept expanding and diversifying to accommodate every change in society such as IT applications, diverse populations who preferred online learning, building organizational capacity, and re-designing learning spaces for effective, efficient quality instruction to all types of learners (Linder, 2017; Mitchell et al., 2017). Likewise, instructional design competencies have also grown merging and overlapping with each other creating a disconnect between how institutions define instructional design versus how instructional designers define their roles and functions. These diverse perspectives are explored further in the following section.

Instructional Design Themes

Most instructional design scholarship and research describes instructional design function and roles as help and support and not as learning design expertise (Council of Regional Accrediting Commission [C-RAC], 2009; Fredericksen, 2017; Halupa, 2019; Mitchell et al., 2017). Instructional design is typically defined as assisting faculty in design and development of courses (Morrison et al., 2019; Russ-Eft, 2013). The importance accorded to instructional design and its practitioners is heavily influenced by how the university or college defines instructional design, functions, and roles. In this section, I synthesize and present major themes stemming from empirical research on instructional design.

Instructional Designer Academic Background vs Experience

Academic degree, certification, and training as an instructional designer, IT professional, or curriculum developer were considerations for instructional design employment and career advancement. Instructional designers with a graduate degree in instructional design were usually preferred to instructional designers who had only a bachelor's degree (Beirne & Romanoski, 2018; Berrett, 2016; Intentional Futures, 2016). Instructional designers with a master's and/or doctorate degree in instructional design, education, or IT occupied positions of mid-level seniority compared to those who did not have an instructional design or education graduate degree. Further, the level of academic expertise was strengthened by relevant certifications in graphic design, eLearning, instructional design theory, training, and evaluation. For example, in her study Ashbaugh (2011) observed that instructional designers with graduate degrees in instruction design or any of the STEM fields (science, technology, engineering, and math) were employed as mid-level informal online leaders. Professionals with bachelor's degrees in instructional design, education, journalism, management, English, and Communication were employed as entry- and junior-level instructional designers. Professionals with a doctoral degree in instructional design, education, and/or IT occupy curriculum development and learning leadership positions.

However, in some cases, curriculum design directors compensated for their lack of a doctoral degree by their years of experience. For example, in their survey Intentional Futures (2016) noted that many curriculum design directors did not have a doctoral degree but had been working in the university for more than 12 years. These directors had joined the university as entry curriculum writers, junior instructional designers, and/or IT assistants and had slowly progressed to director positions. Further, relevant certifications, training, and diplomas in instructional design, graphic design, and eLearning helped instructional designers advance in their careers from junior to mid-level, or from mid-level to director positions (Intentional Futures, 2016; Park & Luo, 2017). Hence, academic and work experience background shaped how instructional designers approached their work—whether they shouldered additional responsibilities and cut across interdepartmental channels to help and support faculty and students. Academic background and experience also helped instructional designers understand and define the nature, scope, and function of instructional design, and its various dimensions. For example, in their survey, Anderson et al. (2019) noted that an understanding of instructional design and competencies enabled instructional designers to identify their roles, functions, value, and position in the university.

Instructional Designer Personal Values

Apart from the strong influences of academic background, and experience, (Larson & Lockee, 2004) the role of personal values, ethics, motivation, and emotions was also paramount in directing instructional designer thought, behavior, and function (Ashbaugh, 2011; Ashbaugh, 2013a, 2013b; Gardner et al., 2018;

Park & Luo, 2017). How instructional designers responded to situations, projects, interactions, faculty, staff, and students depended on personality attributes of empathy, openness, transparency, and resilience. For instance, an instructional designer who understood what expectations, anxiety a new faculty member was facing was more likely to converse frequently, be open, and discuss how to develop instruction from course content and develop rapport (Ashbaugh, 2013a, 2013b). In other instances, instructional designers were able to bounce back even when their suggestions and feedback were viewed in a negative manner.

Personal values of diligence and motivation shaped instructional designer tasks of solving quality issues in course development design, revision of course projects, and collaborating with faculty to plan and conduct learner needs analysis and piloting courses (Park & Luo, 2017). Personal values of self-discipline, trust, respect, and tolerance directed how instructional designers conducted workshops and helped faculty write learning and performance objectives, and assessments, network and coach faculty and IT staff about best learning models and technological software (Ashbaugh, 2011; Ashbaugh, 2013a, 2013b). To quote, personal work ethics of helping, sharing, time-management, and prioritizing tasks enabled instructional designers to *"initiating or participating in educational research, educating faculty about optimal design, mentoring junior IDs, and conducting workshops/ seminars/training sessions"* (Park & Luo, 2017, p. 92).

Likewise, personal characteristics of moral purpose, honesty, and truthfulness were considered important attributes for an instructional designer (Boling et al., 2017; Campbell et al., 2009; Gardner et al., 2018; Gray et al., 2015). Such personal values and emotions were subjective and influenced how an instructional designer approached, valued, and recognized their work, organizational contribution, and ownership of functions and tasks. For example, instructional designers with a high level of moral purpose approached their tasks whether it was course writing, researching best practices, or working with staff to solve LMS problems with sincerity and honesty (Campbell et al., 2009; Gray et al., 2015). Such instructional designers practiced a high moral code characterized by trust, efficiency, civility, and hard work. In another instance, Gardner et al. (2018) discussed how values of belonging, empathy, and teamwork developed a culture of employee empowerment and goodwill.

Institutionally Defined Instructional Designer Roles

Within the institutional context, instructional designers are defined as course design faculty support and IT help staff (Drysdale, 2018, 2019; Macpherson & Smith, 1998; Moskal, 2012; Roberts et al., 1994). As *course design support staff*, instructional designers functioned as researchers, course writers, and proofreaders with skills of communication, collaboration, teamwork, and advisement (Knight & Trowler, 2000; Macpherson & Smith, 1998; Roberts et al., 1994). In some universities they were course librarians with functions of training, and mentoring faculty on how to design courses. They also helped faculty, leadership, and staff in differentiating between long-term learning curricula and short-term training programs and conducting training workshops on grammar and writing style (Allen, 1996; Moskal, 2012). Similarly, Drysdale (2018) said that instructional designers who participated in his doctoral research performed tasks of course writing, content review, research, and mentoring. A follow-up research study added a further dimension of ensuring that student needs, expectations, and demands were realized in the curriculum (Drysdale, 2019). In their study Gray et al. (2015) explained that the support function referred to helping faculty plan and prioritize curriculum goals. For instance, instructional designers wrote learning and performance objectives, course introductions, class activities for online, and hybrid courses to assist faculty. Boling et al. (2017) in her research described the support function as being responsive to people and situations. She stated that instructional designers collaborated and networked with faculty and leadership to design and improve curriculum design systems.

In other universities, instructional designers were described as *IT, and multi-media help* (Hansen, 2010; Iqdami & Branch, 2016; Kang & Ritzhaupt, 2015; Kumar & Ritzhaupt, 2017; Park & Luo, 2017; Ritzhaupt & Kumar, 2015; Sharif & Cho, 2015). In his quantitative study which coded and analyzed 178 instructional design job descriptions, Hansen (2010) found that more than 77% of instructional design jobs in higher education institutions focused on aspects of incorporating, updating, and maintaining websites. Other functions included developing, publishing, embedding videos, and interactive presentations using appropriate educational technology software. Instructional designers were also responsible for LMS technical checks to ensure efficient and smooth operation of online and hybrid courses. Instructional designers were tasked with answering questions about technical issues in uploading courses, online grading, and assessment mechanisms (Kang & Ritzhaupt, 2015; Ritzhaupt & Kumar, 2015; Sharif & Cho, 2015). The technical eLearning role of instructional designers encompassed multi-media skills of using audio and video cloud software applications to write interactive course content and assessments, updating, and developing courses to match web accessibility standards as sanctioned by ADA. This included checking font, color and grammar of courses, creating closed or open captions, and regulating copyright from appropriate educational authorities (Iqdami & Branch, 2016).

Another function of the IT help role included functions of resource allocation of university physical, human, and financial resources, and supervision, coordination of small- and large-scale curriculum development and design projects (Allen, 1996; Cox & Osguthorpe, 2003; McDaniel & Liu, 1996; Moskal, 2012; Surry & Robinson, 2001; Van Rooij, 2010, 2011; Yang et al., 1995). Instructional designers organized subject-matter content embedded with graphic design elements into weekly instructional materials through e-storyboards. They helped faculty select appropriate learner-oriented educational technology software.

Influence of Institutional Context and Culture on Instructional Designer Roles

Another common theme which emerged from several research studies is the strong influence of institution structure and the organizational climate and culture on the roles and activities of instructional designers (Acevedo & Roque, 2019; Hansen, 2010; Knight & Trowler, 2000; Miller & Stein, 2016; Richardson et al., 2019). Institutional structure and culture refer to how the university is structured and organized. Is it a bureaucracy with multiple layers of hierarchy, or is it a team structure? Is the university centralized with a common mission and goal and executive leadership personnel, or is it decentralized with many colleges and administrative units? What effect does the university structure have on university culture?

Hierarchical Structures

University structures with multiple levels of hierarchy shape how instructional designers perform their tasks and functions. In his analysis of 178 job descriptions of instructional designers in decentralized universities, Hansen (2010) found that instructional designers were positioned on a low hierarchy within the organizational structure. Instructional designers were part of the main university campus but kept apart in a separate location such as in the IT maintenance office, library, or in a separate office building. Instructional designers, therefore, did not feel a part of the university and felt marginalized and sidelined. The result of this physical separation was that instructional designers did not feel that their role and function contributed to university productivity and performance. They had poor levels of belonging and ownership of a course design project. Instructional designer roles did not extend beyond their limited function of help and assistance in course design and IT. Involvement in the evaluation, implementation, and delivery of the instruction was not encouraged or formally defined in the instructional designer job description. More than 77% of instructional design jobs recognized instructional design work as that of IT, updating university and library websites with the latest information, and ensuring the smooth functioning of LMS. Hence, the hierarchical university structure relegated instructional designer professionals to IT staff positions who were mere helpers of faculty and did not have their own identity in the university setting.

Similar research findings showed that decentralized university settings with multiple layers of hierarchy confined instructional designers as

IT multi-media staff (Lowell & Ashby, 2018 Iqdami & Branch, 2016; Kang & Ritzhaupt, 2015; Ritzhaupt & Kumar, 2015; Sharif & Cho, 2015). Decentralized universities positioned instructional designers on a low scale of IT support staff restricting their technical skillset to digital scripting, programming, or writing in code, HTML, and other computer languages (Iqdami & Branch, 2016). Instructional designers worked in silos towards attainment of IT short-term goals such as writing code to override or minimize an LMS technical glitch, uploading courses into the LMS, and developing course shells in the LMS. Instructional designers were not encouraged to have a holistic vision of how courses were going to be received by students, or how courses were going to be piloted. Their vision and position in the hierarchy was myopic (Intentional Futures, 2016; Park & Luo, 2017).

These findings were mirrored in a qualitative study by Drysdale (2018) which explored the impact of institutional structures on instructional designer function and value. Decentralized organizational and departmental structures increased red-tape and formal hierarchical channels. Instructional designers were identified as technical personnel with limited skills of writing, proofreading, and IT troubleshooting. They worked in IT silos and were not involved in the overall design process of any course design and development. In fact, their restrictive status and role defined their role as dispensable; a cog in the mechanistic bureaucracy of the organization (Hupe & Hill, 2007). As such their role resembled that of an assembly line worker who performed functions of writing, proofreading, and IT mindlessly. Drysdale further commented that hierarchical structures led to rigid and controlling cultures of one-way top-down communication. Such institutional and departmental cultures did not encourage fluid lines of collaboration, reporting, and accountability which further restricted creativity and sense of ownership of the course design process. In fact, such hierarchical structures and cultures identified instructional designers as external help and support personnel who did not internalize the course design and development process.

Flat, Team Structures

In contrast, flat, team structures positioned instructional designers as collaborative and strategic partners who mentored, coached, and advised faculty on all aspects of the course design process. Such centralized structures fostered cultures of openness, civility, and distributed leadership (Drysdale, 2018; Trekles, 2011). Instructional designers were responsible for developing campus-wide communities, collaborating with faculty and staff, and developing community initiatives. They networked, supported, shared, and built relationships with different organizational members to create a positive working environment. Team structures had a common mission and vision which simplified organizational norms and protocols and encouraged fluidity and ownership of institutional vision, mission, department goals, and aims. Instructional designers shared equal responsibility of designing, developing, analyzing, and delivering quality online learning experiences. Their role shifted from behind-the-scenes to frontline being in direct contact with internal and external stakeholders (Drysdale, 2018; Intentional Futures, 2016; Miller & Stein, 2016; Park & Luo, 2017). To continue, Drysdale observed that team structures minimized levels of reporting and red tape creating transparent and two-way channels of supervision, and accountability. This minimized duplication of systems and protocols where clients had to approach several departments to get their work done. Open communicative department structures emphasized a feeling of respect and acknowledging each other's professional expertise.

Department Cultures

Department culture framed how curricula development was done by instructional designers. Did they collaborate and engage in fluid smooth consultation with faculty and staff to write, research, organize, and sequence instruction? Or did they follow rigid protocols of hierarchy and formal communication of monthly meetings (Gray et al., 2015; Knight & Trowler, 2000). Findings showed that hierarchical structures fostered a mechanistic stiff culture of minimal open and flexible communication and collaboration. Practices of open door were not encouraged. All minute details had to be entered into formal written reports and meeting protocols creating unnecessary paperwork and discouraging open two-way communication.

Such mechanistic cultural controls were not formalized but practiced in daily life and soon became an established institutional cultural norm. These unwritten organization cultural protocols shaped how instructional designers worked and interacted with faculty, staff, and executive leadership. In fact, the organization norm was to develop a myopic vision to only perform functions listed in the official job descriptions and restrict movement and/or exchange of ideas and information among employees.

Comparatively, Ashbaugh (2011) as part of her doctoral research on instructional designers shed light on the culture of team university settings. She found department cultures in teams followed unwritten institutional norms of openness, positional parity, flexibility, and transparency. To quote, instructional designers "*were integral to the course design, to the student learning, to the outcomes*" (Ashbaugh, 2011, p. 150). As the quote shows, instructional designer roles were considered important for the achievement of institutional and/or organizational vision and mission. Their roles were responsible for the overall course design and development process. Ashbaugh clarified that the primary responsibility of instructional designer was "*mastering online improvements and implementing best practices in developing the engaging, motivating, interactive, and effective learning environments for today's learners*"

(Ashbaugh, 2011, p. 150). This shows that in team cultures, the support role of instructional designers was important in designing, developing, and implementing quality learning solutions. The implementation function was limited to seamless and fluid collaboration, communication, and mentoring. This indicated a fair exchange of information, ideas, advice, as well as the crucial and flexible role instructional designers had in the overall course design process.

Influence of Availability of Resources on Instructional Designer Roles

Several research studies show that availability of institutional resources such as staff, technology applications, LMS authorizations and regular updates, computer hardware, budget, professional development activities of training, workshops, webinars, and seminars influences instructional designer roles and functions (Ashbaugh & Piña, 2014; Gardner et al., 2018; Park & Luo, 2017; Van Rooij, 2010, 2011). However, it is difficult to analyze the influence of finite resources as a separate dimension. According to Ashbaugh and Piña (2014), availability, allocation, and delivery of resources are influenced by type, structure, and culture of a university and/or college. For example, limited access to resources of educational technology and course design such as LMS systems and upgrades, course authoring and multi-media software, curriculum design flows and quality matters research restricted instructional designer curriculum development role. Further, limited access restricted instructional designer creativity, autonomy, and flexibility to implement suggestions to improve course design effectiveness.

Park and Luo (2017) argued for the same in their quantitative study. Findings showed that instructional designer roles were dictated by whether the university was a hierarchy with numerous layers—whether its culture was closed, mechanistic, and rigid. Such contexts and cultures determined what resources would be made available to instructional designers including the process or protocol to be followed to gain access to them. Hierarchical decentralized universities with individual missions and visions had different norms and practices which restricted movement and delivery of resources to instructional designers. They did not have access to human resources, technical software, and budget to ensure effectiveness of the overall course design. Lack of proper unlimited access to IT software, applications, course design blueprints including staff, research, and writing training workshops restricted instructional designers to inflexible roles of writing, proofreading, and IT help.

This affected the skill and mindset of instructional designers causing them to develop feelings of resentment, anger, and passive resistance. In fact, as revealed in the survey findings, lack of ready resources caused instructional designers to play second fiddle to faculty, not get involved, or utilize their vast repertoire of skills and knowledge for overall design to streamline processes and avoid duplication (Intentional Futures, 2016; Park & Luo, 2017). Similarly, in her studies, Van Rooij (2010, 2011) argued that instructional designers had access to only those resources which helped them perform functions of course design support and IT help effectively. Instructional designers had access to resources like LMS tools, course writing software, and industry accessibility guidelines but lacked knowledge and access to organizational planning, budgeting, and evaluation resources. Such limits impacted the ability of instructional designers to streamline, develop, merge design systems for developing effective efficient instruction. In fact, limited resources fostered a myopic vision as instructional designers were not involved in holistic functions of course design, budgeting, and staff management (Moskal, 2012). Instructional designer functions of collaboration and communication on small and large course design projects were subject to rigid supervision, monitoring, and top-down communication. The findings, therefore, furthered the norm of providing limited resources to instructional designers which in turn confined them to rigidly structured roles of support staff.

Meanwhile, as noted by Gardner et al. (2018) in their Delphi study, team structures encouraged open access of resources to instructional designers. Such structures allocated unlimited delivery of all resource types to instructional designers allowing them to perform integral and important roles in supporting overall course design projects. Results showed that instructional designers had easy and flexible access to technical, multi-media, and LMS products which equipped them with the ability to choose appropriate educational technology software for effective course design.

Faculty Perceptions of Instructional Designers

Faculty regards instructional designers as course writing staff responsible for content writing, proofreading, and editing (Allen, 1996; Bawa & Watson, 2017; Intentional Futures, 2016; Macpherson & Smith, 1998; Magruder et al., 2019). Faculty believed that acknowledging and treating instructional designers as their counterparts on an equal footing undermined their role as teaching experts leading to a loss of control over their teaching material, and a personal touch in their course (Ren, 2019; Richardson et al., 2019). Faculty perceived instructional designers as *"IT help"* with functions of LMS troubleshooting, maintenance, and development (Kang & Ritzhaupt, 2015; Ritzhaupt & Kumar, 2015). In other studies, faculty identified instructional designers as eLearning multi-media staff who collaborated with faculty to embed educational technology apps in online courses (Anderson et al., 2019; Uibelhoer, 2020). Instructional designers did not have specific assigned functions. They did odd jobs of helping information technology staff with LMS updates and maintenance. In fact, as pointed out by Anderson et al. (2019) in their study instructional designers wore *"many hats"* and performed IT and graphic design tasks of embedding, uploading, checking for broken links, and *"cleaning up code"* (p. 19).

Conclusion

To summarize, instructional design is a broad and ambiguous profession and practice. The presence of overlapping instructional design competencies creates confusion and a disconnect between how the institution defines instructional designer roles versus how instructional designers define their roles and functions. Instructional design is influenced by instructional designer personal characteristics and has learning design and IT expertise. Meanwhile the institution defines instructional designers as IT help and course design assistants. Instructional designer roles and functions are strongly influenced by institutional structure, culture, and available resources. The academic literature allowed me to develop a holistic outlook of instructional design. It enabled me to go beyond and ask questions corresponding to my themes. How do instructional designers reconcile or balance this disconnect and perform daily tasks and functions? What do they do on the job every day to meet performance goals and individual client needs? What coping mechanism or street-level divergence do they follow? In the following chapter, I discuss the theoretical lens and the research design and methodology I followed to empirically explore the *what and how* of instructional designer street-level divergence in higher education.

References

Acevedo, M. M., & Roque, G. (2019). Resisting the deprofessionalization of instructional design. In Y. Vovides & L. R. Lemus (Eds.), *Optimizing instructional design methods in higher education* (pp. 9–26). IGI Global. https://doi.org/10.4018/978-1-5225-4975-8.ch002

Ali, W. (2020). Online and remote learning in higher education institutes: A necessity in light of COVID-19 pandemic. *Higher Education, 10*(3). https://doi.org/10.5539/hes.v10n3p16

Allen, M. (1996). A profile of instructional designers in Australia. *Distance Education, 17*(1), 7–32. https://doi.org/10.1080/0158791960170103

Anderson, M. C., Love, L. M., & Haggar, F. L. (2019). Looking beyond the physician educator: The evolving roles of instructional designers in medical education. *Medical Science Educator, 29*(2), 507–513. https://doi.org/10.1007/s40670-019-00720-6

Annand, D., & Jensen, T. (2017). Incentivizing the production and use of open educational resources in higher education institutions. *International Review of Research in Open and Distributed Learning, 18*(4), 1–15. https://doi.org/10.19173/irrodl.v18i4.3009

Ashbaugh, M. L. (2011). *Online pedagogical quality questioned: Probing instructional designers' perceptions of leadership competencies critical to practice* [Doctoral dissertation, Capella University]. ProQuest. https://www.learntechlib.org/p/118534/

Ashbaugh, M. L. (2013a). Expert instructional designer voices: Leadership competencies critical to global practice and quality online learning designs. *Quarterly Review of Distance Education, 14*(2), 97–118. https://eric.ed.gov/?id=EJ1145200

Ashbaugh, M. L. (2013b). Personal leadership in practice: A critical approach to instructional design innovation work. *Tech Trends, 57*(5), 74–82. https://doi.org/10.1007/s11528-013-0694-5

Ashbaugh, M. L., & Piña, A. A. (2014). Improving instructional design processes through leadership-thinking and modeling. In B. Hokanson & A. Gibbons (Eds.), *Design in educational technology* (pp. 223–247). Springer. https://doi.org/10.1007/978-3-319-00927-8_13

Bawa, P., & Watson, S. (2017). The chameleon characteristics: A phenomenological study of instructional designer, faculty, and administrator perceptions of collaborative instructional design environments. *The Qualitative Report, 22*(9), 2334. https://doi.org/10.46743/2160-3715/2017.2915

Beirne, E., & Romanoski, M. (2018). *Instructional design in higher education: Defining an evolving field.* Online Learning Consortium. https://onlinelearningconsortium.org/read/instructional-design-in-higher-education-defining-an-evolving-field/

Berrett, D. (2016, February 29). Instructional design: Demand grows for a new breed of academic. *The Chronicle of Higher Education. https://www.chronicle.com/article/instructional-design/*

Boling, E., Alangari, H., Hajdu, I. M., Guo, M., Gyabak, K., Khlaif, Z., Kizilboga, R., Tomita, K., Alsaif, M., Lachheb, A., Bae, H., Ergulec, F., Zhu, M., Basdogan, M., Buggs, C., Sari, A., & Techawitthayachinda, R. I. (2017). Core judgments of instructional designers in practice. *Performance Improvement Quarterly, 30*(3), 199–219. https://doi.org/10.1002/piq.21250

Campbell, K., Schwier, R. A., & Kenny, R. F. (2009). The critical, relational practice of instructional design in higher education: An emerging model of change agency. *Educational Technology Research and Development, 57*(5), 645–663. https://doi.org/10.1007/s11423-007-9061-6

Council of Regional Accrediting Commission (C-RAC). (2009). *Guidelines for the evaluation of distance education (on-line learning).* Higher Learning Commission (HLC): A Commission of the North Central Association. https://download.hlcommission.org/C-RAC_Distance_Ed_Guidelines_7_31_2009.pdf

Cowan, S. (2020, March 16). *How to lead in a crisis.* Chronicle of Higher Education. https://www.chronicle.com/article/how-to-lead-in-a-crisis/

Cox, S., & Osguthorpe, R. T. (2003). How do instructional design professionals spend their time? *TechTrends, 47*(3), 45–47. https://doi.org/10.1007/BF02763476

Dick, W. (1996). The Dick and Carey model: Will it survive the decade? *Educational Technology Research and Development, 44*(3), 55–63. https://doi.org/10.1007/BF02300425

Dick, W., Carey, L., & Carey, J. O. (2005). *The systematic design of instruction* (6th ed.). Longman.

Dijkstra, S. (2001). The design space for solving instructional design problems. *Instructional Science, 29*(4–5), 275–290. https://doi.org/10.1023/A:1011939724818

Drysdale, J. (2018). *The organizational structures of instructional design teams in higher education: A multiple case study* [Doctoral dissertation, Abilene Christian University]. Digital Commons @ ACU. https://digitalcommons.acu.edu/etd

Drysdale, J. (2019). The collaborative mapping model: Relationship-centered instructional design for higher education. *Online Learning, 23*(3), 56–71. https://doi.org/10.24059/olj.v23i3.2058

Edmondson, A. C. (2020, March 6). Don't hide bad news in times of crisis. *Harvard Business Review.* https://hbr.org/2020/03/dont-hide-bad-news-in-times-of-crisis

Fernandez, A. A., & Shaw, G. P. (2020). Academic leadership in a time of crisis: The coronavirus and COVID-19. *Journal of Leadership Studies, 14*(1), 39–45. https://doi.org/10.1002/jls.21684

Fox, K., Bryant, G., Lin, N., & Srinivasa, N. (2020). *Time for Class–COVID-Part 1: A national survey of faculty during COVID-19.* Tyton & Partners. https://www.everylearnereverywhere.org/resources/time-for-class-covid-19-edition/

Fredericksen, E. E. (2017). A national study of online learning leaders in US higher education. *Online Learning, 21*(2), n2. https://doi.org/10.24059/olj.v21i2.1164

Gardner, J., Chongwony, L., & Washington, T. (2018). Investigating instructional design management and leadership competencies–A delphi study. *Online Journal of Distance Learning Administration, 21*(1), 1–21. https://eric.ed.gov/?id=EJ1173467

Gray, C. M., Dagli, C., Demiral-Uzan, M., Ergulec, F., Tan, V., Altuwaijri, A. A., Gyabak, K., Hilligoss, M., Kizilboga, R., & Tomita, K. (2015). Judgment and instructional design: How ID practitioners work in practice. *Performance Improvement Quarterly, 28*(3), 25–49. https://doi.org/10.1002/piq.21198

Gustafson, K. L., & Branch, R. M. (2002). *Survey of instructional development models* (4th ed.). ERIC.

Halupa, C. (2019). Differentiation of roles: Instructional designers and faculty in the creation of online courses. *International Journal of Higher Education, 8*(1), 55–68. https://doi.org/10.5430/ijhe.v8n1p55

Hansen, B. E. (2010). *Characteristics of context for instructional design* (Publication Number 041) [Doctoral dissertation, Capella University]. ProQuest.

Hardré, P. (2005). A case for instructional design as a professional development tool-of-choice for university teaching assistance. *Innovative Higher Education, 11*, 16–30. https://doi.org/10.1007/s10755-005-6301-8

Hupe, P., & Hill, M. (2007). Street-Level bureaucracy and public accountability. *Public Administration, 85*(2), 279–299. https://doi.org/10.1111/j.1467-9299.2007.00650.x

Intentional Futures. (2016). *Instructional design in higher education: A report on the role, workflow, and experience of instructional designers.* https://uploads-ssl.webflow.com/61bb092a5c21437cb3a10798/624241a510e63d6f7eee6cd0_Instructional-Design-in-Higher-Education-Report.pdf

International Board of Standards for Performance, Training, & Instruction. (2000). *Instructional design competencies report.* IBSTPI. https://ibstpi.org/competency-sets-services/instructional-designer-competencies/

Iqdami, M. N., & Branch, R. M. (2016). Examining multimedia competencies for educational technologists in higher education. *TechTrends, 60*(4), 365–373. https://doi.org/10.1007/s11528-016-0064-1

Kang, Y. J., & Ritzhaupt, A. D. (2015). A job announcement analysis of educational technology professional positions: Knowledge, skills, and abilities. *Journal of Educational Technology Systems, 43*(3), 231–256. https://doi.org/10.1177/0047239515570572

Knight, P. T., & Trowler, P. R. (2000). Department-level cultures and the improvement of learning and teaching. *Studies in Higher Education, 25*(1), 69–83. https://doi.org/10.1080/030750700116028

Koszalka, T. A., RussEft, D. F., & Reiser, R. (2013). *Instructional designer competencies: The standards* (4th ed.). IAP.

Kumar, S., & Ritzhaupt, A. (2017). What do instructional designers in higher education really do? *International Journal on E-Learning, 16*(4), 371–393. https://eric.ed.gov/?id=EJ1155226

Larson, M. B., & Lockee, B. B. (2004). Instructional design practice: Career environments, job roles, and a climate of change. *Performance Improvement Quarterly, 17*(1), 22–40. https://doi.org/10.1111/j.1937-8327.2004.tb00300.x

Linder, K. D. S., M.E. (2017). Research preparation and engagement of instructional designers in U.S. higher education. O. L. Consortium. https://onlinelearningconsortium.org/

Lowell, V. L., & Ashby, I. V. (2018). Supporting the development of collaboration and feedback skills in instructional designers. *Journal of Computing in Higher Education, 30*(1), 72–92. https://doi.org/10.1007/s12528-018-9170-8

Macpherson, C., & Smith, A. (1998). Academic authors' perceptions of the instructional design and development process for distance education: A case study. *Distance Education, 19*(1), 124–141. https://doi.org/10.1080/0158791980190109

Magruder, O., Arnold, D. A., Moore, S., & Edwards, M. (2019). What is an ID? A survey study. *Online Learning, 23*(3), 137–160. https://doi.org/10.24059/olj.v23i3.1546

McDaniel, K., & Liu, M. (1996). A study of project management techniques for developing interactive multimedia programs: A practitioner's perspective. *Journal of Research on Computing in Education, 29*(1), 29–48. https://doi.org/10.1080/08886504.1996.10782185

Merrill, M. D., Drake, L., Lacy, M. J., Pratt, J., & ID2_Research_Group. (1996). Reclaiming instructional design. Educational Technology, 36(5), 5–7.

Miller, S. & Stein, G. (2016). Finding our voice: Instructional designers in higher education. Educause Review. https://er.educause.edu/articles/2016/2/finding-our-voice-instructional-designers-in-higher-education

Mitchell, K., Simpson, C., & Adachi, C. (2017). *What's in a name: The ambiguity and complexity of technology enhanced learning roles* [Conference presentation]. Facilitating social learning through learning design: A perspective of collaborative academic development. https://2017conference.ascilite.org/program/

Morgan, T. (2019). Instructional designers and open education practices: Negotiating the gap between intentional and operational agency. *Open Praxis, 11*(4), 369–380. https://doi.org/10.5944/openpraxis.11.4.1011

Morrison, G. R., Ross, S. M., Kemp, J. E., & Kalman, H. K. (2019). *Designing effective instruction* (6th ed.). John Wiley & Sons.

Moskal, T. M. (2012). *Instructional designers in higher education* [Doctoral dissertation, University of Nebraska-Lincoln]. http://digitalcommons.unl.edu/cehsedaddiss/121

Munzenmaier, C. (2014). *Today's instructional designer: Competencies and careers* (Perspectives, Issue). https://www.learningguild.com/insights/178/todays-instructional-designer-competencies-and-careers/

Namatherdhala, B., Mazher, N., & Sriram, G. K. (2022). A comprehensive overview of artificial intelligence trends in education. *International Research Journal of Modernization in Engineering Technology and Science*, 4 (7). pp. 1261–1264

Oliver, M. (2002). What do learning technologists do? Innovations in Education and Teaching International, 39(4), 45–252. https://doi.org/10.1080/13558000210161089

Park, J.-Y., & Luo, H. (2017). Refining a competency model for instructional designers in the context of online higher education. *International Education Studies, 10*(9), 87–98. https://doi.org/10.5539/ies.v10n9p87

Perez, R. S., & Emery, C. D. (1995). Designer thinking: How novices and experts think about instructional design. *Performance Improvement Quarterly, 8*(3), 80–95. https://doi.org/10.1111/j.1937-8327.1995.tb00688.x

Pilbeam, R. (2021, March 4). *The COVID-19 wake up call: Instructional designers are key to creating accessible and inclusive learning models*. The evoLLLution, a modern campus initiative. https://evolllution.com/programming/program_planning/the-covid-19-wake-up-call-instructional-designers-are-key-to-creating-accessible-and-inclusive-learning-models/

Reigeluth, C., Watson, S. L., Watson, W., Dutta, P., Zengguan, C., & Powell, N. (2008). Roles for technology in the information-age paradigm of education. *Learning Management Systems, 48*(6), 32–40. https://eric.ed.gov/?id=EJ829867

Reiser, R. A. (2001a). A history of instructional design and technology: Part I: A history of instructional media. *Educational Technology Research and Development, 49*(1), 53. https://doi.org/10.1007/BF02504506

Reiser, R. A. (2001b). A history of instructional design and technology: Part II: A history of instructional design. *Educational Technology Research and Development, 49*(2), 57–67. https://doi.org/10.1007/BF02504928

Reiser, R. A., & Dempsey, J. V. (2012). *Trends and issues in instructional design and technology* (R. A. Reiser & J. V. Dempsey, Eds., 3rd ed.). Pearson.

Ren, X. (2019). The undefined figure: Instructional designers in the Open Educational Resource (OER) movement in higher education. *Education and Information Technologies, 24*(6), 3483–3500. https://doi.org/10.1007/s10639-019-09940-0

Richardson, J. C., Ashby, I., Alshammari, A. N., Cheng, Z., Johnson, B. S., Krause, T. S., Lee, D., Randolph, A. E., & Wang, H. (2019). Faculty and instructional designers on building successful collaborative relationships. *Educational Technology Research and Development, 67*(4), 855–880. https://doi.org/10.1007/s11423-018-9636-4

Richey, R. C., Fields, D. C., & Foxon, M. (2001). *Instructional design competencies: The standards* (3rd ed.). ERIC.

Ritzhaupt, A. D., & Kumar, S. (2015). Knowledge and skills needed by instructional designers in higher education. *Performance Improvement Quarterly, 28*(3), 51–69. https://doi.org/10.1002/piq.21196

Roberts, D. W., Jackson, K., Osborne, J., & Vine, A. S. (1994). Attitudes and perceptions of academic authors to the preparation of distance education materials at the university of Tasmania. *Distance Education, 15*(1), 70–93. https://doi.org/10.1080/0158791940150106

Russ-Eft, D. F., Bober, M. J., De La Teja, I., Foxon, M., & Koszalka, T. A. (2013). *Evaluator competencies: Standards for the practice of evaluation in organizations* (Vol. 22). John Wiley & Sons.

Seels, B., & Glasgow, Z. (1998). *Making instructional design decisions*. Merrill.

Seels, B. B., & Richey, R. C. (2012). *Instructional technology: The definition and domains of the field* (1994 edition ed.). IAP.

Sharif, A., & Cho, S. (2015). 21st-century instructional designers: Bridging the perceptual gaps between identity, practice, impact and professional development. *International Journal of Educational Technology in Higher Education, 12*(3), 72–85. https://doi.org/10.7238/rusc.v12i3.2176

Shearer, R. (2003). Instructional design in distance education: An overview. In M. G. M. W. G. Anderson (Ed.), *Handbook of distance education* (2nd ed., pp. 275–286). Lawrence Erlbaum Associates. 10.1016/j.iheduc.2003.08.002

Short, D. C., & Shindell, T. J. (2009). Defining HRD scholar practitioners. *Advances in Developing Human Resources*, *11*(4), 472–485. https://doi.org/10.1177/1523422309342225

Sims, R. C., & Koszalka, T. A. (2008). Competencies for the new-age instructional designer. In M. D. M. J. M. Spector, J. van Merrienboer, and M. P. Driscoll (Eds.), *Handbook of research on educational communications and technology* (3rd ed., pp. 569–575). Lawrence Erlbaum.

Smith, P. L., & Ragan, T. J. (2004). *Instructional design*. John Wiley & Sons.

Surry, D. W., & Robinson, M. A. (2001). A taxonomy of instructional technology service positions in higher education. *Innovations in Education and Teaching International*, *38*(3), 231–238. https://doi.org/10.1080/14703290110051406

Trekles, A. M. (2011). *University instructional designers: Everyday leadership in the age of accountability*. ERIC. https://files.eric.ed.gov/fulltext/ED543913.pdf

Uibelhoer, D. (2020). *Practicing what they preach: A case study exploring the experiences of instructional designers as educators of an online teaching certificate program* [Doctoral dissertation, Ston Hall University]. https://scholarship.shu.edu/dissertations/2829/

Van Rooij, S. W. (2010). Project management in instructional design: ADDIE is not enough. *British Journal of Educational Technology*, *41*(5), 852–864. https://doi.org/10.1111/j.1467-8535.2009.00982.x

Van Rooij, S. W. (2011). Instructional design and project management: Complementary or divergent? *Educational Technology Research and Development*, *59*(1), 139–158. https://doi.org/10.1007/S11423-010-9176-Z

Vovides, Y., & Lemus, L. R. (2019). The evolving landscape of instructional design in higher education. In *Optimizing instructional design methods in higher education* (pp. 1–8). IGI Global. https://doi.org/10.4018/978-1-5225-4975-8.ch001

Xie, J., Gulinna, A., & Rice, M. F. (2021). Instructional designers' roles in emergency remote teaching during COVID-19. *Distance Education*, *42*(1), 70–87. https://doi.org/10.1080/01587919.2020.1869526

Yang, C.-S., Moore, D. M., & Burton, J. K. (1995). Managing courseware production: An instructional design model with a software engineering approach. *Educational Technology Research and Development*, *43*(4), 60–70. https://doi.org/10.1007/BF02300491

3 Theory and Design

Every research endeavor needs a theoretical underpinning that allows a researcher to anchor their assumptions and hypothesis, investigate, and evaluate and assess whether the assumptions put forth by them are valid or not (Bond & Dirkin, 2018; Brodkin, 2011). As such, research investigations are conceived with assumptions and a dilemma in mind and then molded within a theory to provide a firm foundation. This foundation enables a scientific empirical investigation followed by critical evaluation, conclusions, and recommendations. This research investigation explores the assumption that instructional designers act as street-level bureaucrats to deal with the daily conflict and dilemma of job roles and function vs bending departmental policy norms to achieve learner/consumer satisfaction. Do they develop *flexible rules of thumb* to achieve goals of designing learner-oriented instruction and streamline design processes? To quote, instructional designers "*have responsibility for making unique and fully appropriate responses to individual clients and their situations*" (Lipsky, 1980, p. 161).

Street-Level Bureaucracy (SLB)

I anchored my assumptions of instructional designer behavior on the theoretical foundation or underpinning of street-level bureaucracy (SLB), a sociological theory that explains how frontline workers in public services such as welfare, policing, and education enact organizational policies and functions in their daily routine work (Lipsky, 1980). The theory is based on the foundational assumption that frontline workers such as teachers, social workers, judges, public lawyers, and police officers who have direct contact with clients are street-level bureaucrats (Davidovitz & Cohen, 2022; Magnusson, 1981). The theory discusses how daily practical functions of a job differ from official job descriptions causing frontline professionals to face difficulties on the job (Moore, 1987). The theory describes how frontline street-level bureaucrats develop coping mechanisms to successfully meet and overcome these difficulties. Each street-level bureaucrat develops a coping mechanism identified as *street-level divergence* or striking a balance between *citizen-agent narrative* and *state-agent narrative* (Cooper et al., 2015; Destler, 2017; Frisch Aviram et al., 2021; Lipsky, 2010; Maynard-Moody et al., 2003). The agent is the street-level bureaucrat, while the citizen is the client, and the state is the institution. The theory, therefore, explains how the agent views state and citizen narrative to intersect with their own narrative and develops the coping mechanism of street-level divergence.

The theory, therefore, structured my study and set boundaries. It enabled me to focus on university outlined job functions and instructional designer perceptions about their functions, institutional systems, structure, and culture. The theory helped me determine if there was indeed a gap between official job functions and instructional designer perceptions of what they did on the job that produced conflict for the instructional designer. The theory also helped me determine whether instructional designers developed coping mechanisms to address conflict.

SLB theory comprises two dimensions of macro and micro, which, when combined, lead to SLB behavior, i.e., street-level divergence. Each dimension branches into defining features. The macro dimension has three elements or job goals. The micro dimension has three narratives or perspectives, and each narrative comprises elements. As such, a frontline employee must deal with three narratives of state, agent, and client. The state narrative is equated with an institutional perspective. Agent narrative: in this study, the agent was the instructional designer from the perspective of the frontline employee. In my study, the instructional designer was the agent who viewed the state or institution narrative and balanced it with the narrative of the client or citizen, i.e., faculty, staff, and learners, to perform daily job functions. Instructional designers, therefore, had three perspectives or narratives: (a) agent narrative which was their personal values, knowledge, experiences, and training; (b) institutional narrative of instructional designer jobs and functions, and how the institution framed them; and c) client narrative which was how faculty, staff, and learners viewed instructional designer roles and daily functions. The interaction of these three narratives enabled instructional designers to develop street-level divergence. For example, how do institutional narrative factors intersect and impact instructional designer factors to develop the coping behavior of street-level divergence? And how does this coping behavior of street-level divergence enable instructional designers to achieve the job goals under macro dimension? The sections below provide a breakdown of the SLB theory.

Macro Dimension

This dimension of SLB constitutes the broad overarching elements of the theory. The macro dimension, also known as *organizational contribution*, has three elements: (a) performing official job duties, (b) meeting client expectations, and (c) contributing to organizational development and performance. These three elements are identified as the three goals of a job. Job goals usually determine when and how frontline employees exercise coping behaviors to deal with on-the-job conflict. For instance, frontline employees improvise and bend rules of institutional systems when institutional structures and cultures curb autonomy and constrain meeting diverse client needs and making decisions (Frisch Aviram, 2021). Thus, coping and working around and bending rules could be a necessary response by frontline employees when faced with a toxic organizational culture, limited and insufficient resources, and ambiguous client needs (e.g., not knowing that the client wants) (Cooper, 2015; Lipsky, 2010). But it is not necessarily a feasible way for an organization to operate though such street-level behavior might be providing ways to meet job goals.

Micro Dimension

The micro dimension is the primary component of the SLB theory. It compromises three narratives or perspectives. Agent or instructional designer perspective is not visible but influences the other perspectives of the micro dimension. State or institutional perspective forms the other narrative followed by the client or faculty and learner narrative. Each narrative is broken down into minute elements which frame, intersect, and influence how instructional designers behave and act on the job to achieve the three job goals of organizational contribution of the macro dimension.

Institutional/University Narrative

This narrative constitutes three elements known as the *framing factors*: (a) institutional context and culture, (b) finite resources, and (c) ambiguous client expectations. These three framing factors structure university perceptions of instructional designer roles and functions. The university narrative intersects with instructional designer narrative to form street-level divergent behaviors of instructional designers. In this study, I investigated how instructional designers viewed their official functions and roles, and the institutional framing factors as discussed in the sections below.

Institutional Context and Culture

This factor refers to the physical systems and structures of the institution (Lipsky, 1980). Is the institution a pyramid-layered hierarchy or is it a flat team-based structure where all employees irrespective of their functions hold equal status?

A twin element of institutional and department culture influences job structures, functions, and employee interactions (Davidovitz & Cohen, 2022;

Hupe & Hill, 2007). Jobs in flexible structures and cultures enable development of fluid jobs built on principles of trust, participation, collaboration, and accountability. To quote, employees working in such institutional cultures do not become *"cogs in a complex, mechanistic system, rather workers who are able to exert autonomy and bring creativity to their tasks"* (Hupe & Hill, 2007, p. 167). However, jobs in hierarchical structures with rigid mechanistic culture are closed and narrow and do not encourage participation, openness, and trust.

Finite Resources

This factor refers to finite limited supply of resources vs unlimited, as well as increasing demand for resources and services (Frisch Aviram et al., 2021; Keiser, 2010). In other words, it means having demand more than supply of manpower, physical resources, and budgetary considerations. Job roles and functions are influenced by how much resource supply the institution has and whether is it enough to meet and satisfy clientele demands and expectations. Frontline employees who enjoy open communication and participation tend to share a finite supply of resources to meet unlimited client demand.

Ambiguous Client Expectations

Institutional jobs exist to fulfill and satisfy client needs and expectations (Howard, 2017; Jones, 2001). This is easy and linear if all clients had the same expectations, needs, and demands. However, this does not happen. Each client has a unique background and situation that makes every expectation different and individualistic. Multiple clients with individualistic diverse needs and expectations confuse job functions and responsibilities.

Agent/Instructional Designer Narrative

This narrative or perspective is an integral part of how the instructional designer views and perceives institutional/university and client/learner and faculty narratives. Instructional designer narratives comprise instructional designer academic knowledge, skills, experience, training, personal values, ethics, and motivations (Moore, 1987). Understanding instructional designer narrative is critical in finding out how instructional designers balance their narrative with those of the university. For this study I focused on finding out the academic background, personal characteristics of instructional designers, as well as the factors which influenced their exercise of street-level divergence.

Professionalism

This characteristic includes codes of conduct, training, and experience (Cooper et al., 2015; Evans, 2010; Fisher, 1986). It also includes individual personal characteristics of likes, dislikes, beliefs, values, and mindsets. Street-level bureaucrats rely on their subject knowledge, training, skillset, and attitude when choosing, prioritizing, and performing daily job tasks.

Flexible Decision-Making

This characteristic refers to the extent to which street-level bureaucrats exercise personal discretion to make decisions, provide support, adjust, and improvise on the job (Frisch Aviram et al., 2021; Gofen, 2014; Loyens & Maesschalck, 2010). Also known as discretionary flexibility, the characteristic is apparent when there is an inadequate supply of resources, competing ambiguous client needs and a rigid, mechanistic institutional context. Comparatively, frontline employees in flexible institutional systems tend to exercise discretion and choice when sharing limited resources and interacting collaboratively to meet client needs.

Autonomy

This characteristic is related to flexible decision-making and refers to an ill-defined process of *bending and breaking the rules* to make decisions and perform job functions (Brodkin, 2011; Cooper, 2015; Gofen, 2014). Autonomy means being able to modify job descriptions to join objectives with available resources to provide support and network with clients and bridge the gap between goals and needs. Frontline employees in open and flexible systems tend to have more autonomy than employees in hierarchical closed systems. This is because open systems encourage direct interactions and teamwork as compared to closed systems which are characterized by rigid hierarchies and minimal interaction.

Employee Engagement

Also identified as trust, this characteristic refers to the degree of belonging and ownership frontline employees experience in their job (Davidovitz & Cohen, 2022; Evans & Harris, 2004; Loyens & Maesschalck, 2010). Higher levels of trust and respect mean a greater likelihood that frontline employees conform to institutional job descriptions. Frontline employees in centralized institutions characterized by flexibility and openness tend to experience engagement as these institutions invest in *professional development activities* such as organizing refresher workshops and career seminars. How do instructional designers develop trust, ownership, and belonging when they work in silos and are not involved in entire course design projects.

Client/Faculty and Learner Narrative

Client or citizen narrative comprises how internal university clients like faculty, learners, and staff view instructional designer roles and functions. Exploring client narrative is understanding how instructional designer narrative intersects with diverse client needs and expectations and influences instructional designers in prioritizing and organizing their tasks (Maynard-Moody et al., 2003). For this study, client narrative was explored from an instructional designer perspective. It overlapped with characteristics of street-level divergence, that is, communication, flexible decision-making, collaboration, and autonomy.

Research Design/Methodology

Methodology or design is described as the scientific method or way wherein an individual approaches a problem and seeks answers (Merriam & Tisdell, 2015). Methodology is an individual's research paradigm and worldview comprising their assumptions, biases, interests, and purposes. Whether we are grappling with everyday dilemmas or scientific research issues and problems, a definitive research design is basic in guiding us to a solution and recommendation involves how we view the world and what we think is important and true (Patton, 2015; Yin, 2016). There are two main research paradigms of positivism or quantitative vs interpretivism/constructivism. Positivism is based on the caveat that all knowledge is neutral and measurable, i.e., any activity which is quantifiable. Subsequently knowledge or thoughts that cannot be observed and measured are of little or no importance. As such it relies on quantifiable/measurable methods of data collection. Examples include surveys and experiments which are devoid of human subjectivities.

In contrast, the paradigm of interpretivism/constructivism believes that knowledge and reality are subjective, multiple, and socially constructed. This paradigm leans towards qualitative data collection methods which explore human behaviors and interactions. Qualitative research focuses on quality and is internal to human experience. Qualitative research leans towards subjective human emotions, moods, and "*internal ideas, feelings, and motives*" (Merriam & Tisdell, 2015).

As per my research paradigm of constructivism, I opted for a qualitative research design which allowed me the opportunity to explore, study, and critically evaluate my three research themes of (a) finding out how instructional designer perceptions of their roles and functions compared to those as outlined in institutional job descriptions, (b) how instructional designers exercised street-level divergence, and (c) how instructional designers contributed to organizational development (Merriam & Tisdell, 2015). I believe that knowledge and reality are not uniform but varied, subjective, and emotional. To me knowledge was not an abstract concept which was resident external to the individual. Knowledge and reality were constructed by individuals living and interacting on a social plane. Knowledge and truth, therefore, could not be external to the individual as it was our perspective, our explanation of behavior, interaction, and action.

Qualitative research, although based on robust theoretical and epistemological groundings of social constructivism, is largely driven by research questions and purpose (Annells, 2006; Caelli et al., 2003; Kahlke, 2014; Thorne, 2008). Keeping this rationale in mind, I opted for a basic qualitative design which describes and explores a phenomenon in the words of the individuals experiencing the phenomena (Creswell, 2013; Denzin & Lincoln, 2011; Merriam & Tisdell, 2015; Patton, 2015). Qualitative design aligns with street-level bureaucrat research which also explores multiple perspectives or *"the dilemmas street-level workers encountered in their work, the way they dealt with these dilemmas; and the motives for dealing with the dilemmas"* (Bachman et al., 2017, p. 137). Both design and topic are based on the tenet that truth is multi-faceted and socially constructed. Therefore, to understand *how, what, and why of street-level divergence*, it was important to gather many perceptions and engage in more than one research method.

The distinguishing methodological fluidity and flexibility of the basic qualitative design, known as method slurring which allowed for method triangulation and vivid description of the studied phenomena, suited my research study (Kahlke, 2014, p. 44). Using two methods to gather relevant data enabled me to have a broad outlook and yet remain grounded and close to the data.

Research Quality

The rigor of qualitative research is always to be explored and discussed before even attempting to conduct the research investigation (Krefting, 1991; Lincoln & Guba, 1985; Yin, 2016). This is because qualitative research deals with human interaction which is ambiguous and culpable of change all the time. Researchers opting to conduct qualitative research must be highly aware and cognizant of their methods, biases, and behavior. Research quality in qualitative research deals with truth value or the confidence in a research work (Krefting, 1991; Lincoln & Guba, 1985; Yin, 2016). Truth value or research trustworthiness is established by accurately capturing and reproducing truth from perspectives of participants. It includes strategies a researcher uses to ensure accurate collection, analysis, and meaningful depiction of data. As explained by Yin (2016), a credible research study *"provides assurance that you have properly collected and interpreted the data, so that the finding and the conclusions accurately reflect and represent that world that was studied*" (p. 85). As such, research quality includes credibility, dependability, confirmability, and transferability.

Credibility

Credibility is establishing the truth of the research study's findings. In other words, it means showing that findings are accurate and honest and that findings match reality (Lapan et al., 2012; Merriam & Tisdell, 2016; Yin, 2016). Reality is not universal and absolute and varies according to the participant's perspective. The issue of accurately capturing each participant's voice is particularly challenging if the research involves more than one site and more than ten participants (Cope, 2014; Yin, 2016). To instill credibility, I sought IRB (institutional review board) approval before attempting to conduct an empirical investigation and collect data. This ensured transparency and accountability of all research methods used, including all legal and ethical research practices codified by IRB. I did member-checking which involved sending a copy of the interview transcript to the participants to ensure their perspective had been appropriately captured.

Dependability

Dependability refers to reliability of the research study findings (Lincoln & Guba, 1985). It means consistency of the study, i.e., arriving at similar findings and conclusions if the study is replicated using similar methods, participants, and research context. However, due to subjective humanistic nature of qualitative research, establishing research study consistency becomes problematic (Marshall, 2016). Human reactions and perspectives are always changing, and therefore, it is essential to have a plan to establish research study dependability. The strategies I used were (a) writing a thick, descriptive report of my study which detailed every research protocol allowing for replication, (b) recording all interviews and using a verbatim pragmatic transcription method which accurately captured all verbal and non-verbal participant responses, and (c) being critical and reflective of my own bias as a former instructional designer in higher education and how my positionality would impact my research study.

Confirmability

In qualitative research confirmability means data confirmability or ensuring that the researcher's subjectivity and influence on the data collected and analyzed are minimized (Lapan et al., 2012; Patton, 2015; Shenton, 2004).

Theory and Design

Confirmability involves providing evidence showing the data sources and process of data collection so that readers can support and understand the research conclusion. As such, measures to achieve confirmability included being aware of my positionality and keeping a reflexive journal. A reflexive journal is a journaling diary kept by the researcher to record personal reflections, biases, and ideas (Korstjens & Moser, 2018). I also consciously separated the research findings from the research conclusions. My findings embodied the voice, i.e., words of my participants to show that every finding was rooted in data and not a figment of my imagination (Cope, 2014). This was done by using *"thick, rich quotes"* from participant interviews to explain my findings (p. 2). Another method that I used was having a peer debriefer, who was familiar with instructional design and could advise me about the authenticity and accuracy of everything I wrote (Marshall, 2016).

Transferability

Transferability commonly refers to generalization or external validity which means that the results of a study can be generalized to other samples from the same population (Cope, 2014; Yin, 2016). I achieved transferability by maintaining a thick, rich, descriptive account of my study which included context, background, data collection process, data analysis, and findings (Lapan et al., 2012; Lincoln & Guba, 1985). This ensured that readers understood and related study findings to their own circumstance and context. As explained by Cope (2014), transferability is achieved when *"the results have meaning to individuals not involved in the study and readers can associate the results with their own experiences"* (p. 1). Furthermore, I connected the research findings to my theoretical framework and academic scholarship on instructional design and answered my research questions. This would help readers in other disciplines and fields understand my study.

My Positionality

Also popularly known as bias and subjectivity, positionality colors and shapes all qualitative research tremendously (Creswell & Creswell, 2018; Lapan et al., 2012). It is an individual's inner natural bias that a researcher brings with them, consciously or unconsciously, to the research process. Qualitative research is individualized and unique where the researcher is a data collection tool. The researcher's educational background, professional experience, beliefs, and perspectives influence the study at all stages starting with choice of research topic, literature review content, data collection, sampling, and interpretation. The issue of positionality becomes more important if the researchers and participants have similar educational and professional backgrounds, which for this study is higher education instructional design. Therefore, strategies to mitigate the effects of researcher positionality were built into every stage of research.

Research Assumptions

I am an experienced instructional designer with a master's degree in instructional design and relevant certifications. I have worked in higher education as an instructional and curriculum designer for 11 years. I have engaged in street-level divergent behavior on the job. I have often bent institutional rules, improvised, and cut corners to meet institutional goals of achieving optimal performance, productivity, fulfilling diverse faculty and learner needs, and contributing to organizational development. I knew what instructional design was, instructional design competencies, and its relevance in higher education. As a member of a specialized and skilled professional group, I considered instructional design as the backbone and foundation of all university functions and operations. Instructional designers design learning experiences with relevant educational technology and eLearning apps which help organizations attract and retain diverse learners. At the same time, instructional designers collaborate, train, and mentor faculty and staff on how to write instruction, navigate learning management system (LMS), and distribute resources for design and related activities. Though this insider knowledge and perspective made it easy to understand instructional design academic literature and language, it was a drawback. Being the insider framed my behavior, my reactions, and my interactions. My strong views on instructional design, what instructional designers can do and what they actually do on the job, what I believe to be limits and restrictions on their role, and how they deal with challenges daily influenced my study findings and interpretation.

I assumed (a) instructional designers are street-level bureaucrats, (b) instructional designers contribute to organizational development, (c) instructional designers are not recognized and acknowledged as integral campus personnel, and (d) instructional designers are marginalized on campus. I assumed that every instructional designer working in higher education is a street-level bureaucrat who improvised and bent rules to meet client needs. I regarded instructional designers as integral campus personnel whose expertise was seldom recognized and acknowledged by other campus staff. Instructional designers were specialized personnel with specific competencies and contributed to the organization. Hence, I expected instructional designers to be flexible, bend institutional rules, functions, improvise, and respond to diverse client needs. I expected my participants to feel resentment, bitterness for being marginalized and not being appreciated for their expertise, and a lack of belonging toward the institution. Being the insider who had similar experiences, I enjoyed a comfort level with all my participants. I could sympathize, understand, and relate to their perceptions. Thus, minimizing my bias and striving for an authentic and transparent study was challenging but very necessary.

Being Reflexive

To minimize my bias and to achieve a transparent study, I engaged in reflexivity. Reflexivity is a dynamic process of interaction within and between the researcher and the researched and the data that informs decisions, actions, and interpretations at all stages (Mann, 2011; Tracy, 2019). I kept a reflexive journal throughout my research journey. I wrote all my ideas, thoughts, questions, and reactions experienced during the research process. Writing about my feelings during the research process made me aware of my bias and helped to reduce it.

However, I believe that my positionality as an instructional designer practitioner helped in developing a holistic, rich interpretation and conclusion. Positionality is "*not some kind of virus which contaminates the research. On the contrary, the self is the research tool, and thus intimately connected to the methods we deploy*" (Cousin, 2010, p. 10). I believed my bias helped in gauging, understanding, probing, and sharing participant perspectives.

The Research Process

The steps following the choice of research methodology constitute the completion of research funnel that culminates in data collection, analysis, evaluation, and recommendation. As a qualitative researcher of basic design, I had free rein to mesh and fuse two different qualitative methods to develop a sound understanding of on-the-job behavior of instructional designers in higher education. As my first research method, I used a document analysis method to gather instructional designer job descriptions. This method gave me a broad outlook of how institutions viewed instructional designer roles and functions. As my second research method, I conducted semi-structured interviews with instructional designers. This method enabled gathering of multiple perspectives and understanding of participant views through their own words.

Research Sites

I deliberately chose higher educational institutions where I would find informative participants who would provide me with relevant insights about instructional designer street-level divergence. Furthermore, I selected institutions which were the same and yet different in type and level. In doing so, therefore, I purposefully chose two universities and a regional technical college, all located in different parts of the country. The rationales for my choice were as follows: (a) a college is identified as a higher education institution,

(b) to provide a comprehensive representation of street-level divergence of instructional designers, (c) a mix of centralized and decentralized university/college structures, and (d) institutions which had large, i.e., five or more employees in instructional design or related departments to ensure a minimum positive response rate of at least four to five participants from each institution. The chosen three research institutions were given pseudonyms to preserve privacy.

River University

The first selected higher educational institution was given the pseudonym *River University*. River University is a midwestern midsize four-year and graduate degree granting public research university with approximately 16,000 students and 600 full-time faculty. Though having six academic colleges and 11 non-academic administrative units, the university has a centralized structure. It has a unified executive leadership body with common university policies and protocols. The largest administrative unit on campus is the Office of Instructional Resources (OIR) which houses campus media services (MRC) and the Instructional Design and Access (IDA) units. Both MRC and IDA units are responsible for the university philosophy and vision of applied learning, research, and innovation. The IDA unit is the instructional design and educational technology unit on campus and functions as a resource of course design and instructional technology for all faculty and staff on campus. IDA trains, supports, and mentors faculty, staff, and students at all colleges and administrative units in online learning (OL) and accessibility issues. Currently, the unit has five employees: two instructional designers, two educational technologists, and an LMS coordinator.

Lane University

The second higher education institution was identified by the pseudonym of *Lane University*. Lane University is a large, diverse southeastern public four-year and graduate degree granting university. The university's four academic colleges and 15 non-academic administrative units function independently with minimal unified common policies and mission. The largest administrative department on campus is the distance education (DE) department which currently has 22 personnel comprising 5 instructional designers, 10 OL and training designers, and 7 educational technologists who interact with campus faculty and other staff. These employees work for a scheduled time at an assigned college or unit on campus and are responsible for course design, social and mobile learning, smart classrooms, and LMS facilitation.

End College

End College is a public two-year technical college offering associate degrees, technical certificates, and diploma programs. Located in southeast US, the college has eight academic and three non-academic ones which function independently with separate philosophies and missions. End College, therefore, is known for its technical certification programs, workforce development and training programs, LMS training, and affiliation with the regional hospital's nursing unit. End College has a large OL department which has 17 personnel comprising 7 OL designers, 10 technology and training specialists, all of whom have direct interaction with learners, faculty, and other campus staff. Each employee is responsible for curricula design, instructional technology, including LMS integration in the assigned department.

Sample

I used purposive sampling to select a final sample of 17 OL/technology/instructional design professionals from a sample pool of 44 staff members from IDA (River University), DE department (Lane University), and OL department (End College). Purposive sampling involved selecting those participants who met my sampling criterion and subsequently provided meaningful and relevant information pertinent to my research questions (Marshall, 2016; Patton, 2015). The sampling criteria were as follows:

- Participants were instructional designers, OL designers, educational technologists, or technology and training specialists. The rationale for this criterion was that higher education instructional designers are inclusive of educational technologists, OL, and DE staff (Acevedo & Roque, 2019; Larson & Lockee, 2004; Surry & Robinson, 2001).
- Participants were full-time employees of IDA, DE, and OL departments. The reason for this criterion was that full-time instructional designers are more invested in long-term course development, alignment between educational technology (Alexander et al., 2019). Full-time instructional designers will be able to provide a holistic in-depth view of official systems and culture.

All participants were given pseudonyms for privacy and confidentiality purposes. I provide details of the chosen participants from each of the three institutions below.

River University

Five participants were selected for job description analysis and interview. Four participants were female, and one was a male. Four participants were

Theory and Design 41

White, and one participant was Ethiopian. All five participants were full-time university employees whose clients were faculty and other campus staff. Table 3.1 graphically presents participant information followed by a brief description.

Ann is the OIR director. After a teaching career of 28 years, she joined River University as an instructional designer. She has held the positions of senior instructional designer, IDA manager, and currently department director. *Ann* has a PhD in adult and continuing education and double master's degrees in history and political science. She has multiple certifications in eLearning, Accessibility, Quality Matters (QM), Certified Professional Training Management (CPTM), and assistive technology.

Nan has been the senior instructional designer at IDA for the past three years. *Nan* has a PhD in Teaching and Curriculum and a master's degree in education planning and management. She holds certifications in QM, technology proficiency in PDF and LMS.

Bess is the senior educational technologist at IDA. She has a master's degree in education technology and multiple certifications in LMS cloud technology, content writing, instructional design, and eLearning.

Table 3.1 River University Participants

Pseudonym	Race	Gender	Job Title	Education	Certification
Ann	White	Female	Director, instructional designer	PhD: adult and continuing education M.A.: history, political science	eLearning, Accessibility, QM, CPTM, assistive technology
Nan	Ethiopian	Female	Senior instructional designer	PhD: teaching and curriculum M.A.: education planning and management	QM, technology proficiency: PDF and LMS
Bess	White	Female	Senior educational technologist	M.A.: education technology	LMS cloud, instructional design, eLearning
Kirk	White	Male	Educational technologist	Ed.D.: Edu. leadership [current] M.A.: fine art and new media	User design, technology, game design, expert LMS levels
Ellie	White	Female	LMS coordinator/ educational technologist	B.A.: business management	LMS Blackboard, disability awareness, QM

Kirk is the IDA educational technologist. His work experience includes being an art faculty member, academic content writer, and the CEO of a supermarket. **Kirk** is currently pursuing his Ed.D. in Educational Leadership. He has a master's degree in fine art and new media with certifications in user design, technology, game design, and expert LMS levels in Blackboard and Moodle.

Ellie has been the IDA's LMS specialist for the past eight years. She has a bachelor's degree in business management with certifications in LMS Blackboard, disability awareness, and QM.

Lane University

I selected seven instructional designers for job description analysis and interview. Four participants were female, and three were male. All participants

Table 3.2 Lane University Participants

Pseudonym	Gender	Race	Job Title	Education	Certifications
Chloe	Female	White	Senior instructional designer	B.A.: English	Training, graphic design, LMS proficiency
Paul	Male	White	Instructional designer support	B.A.: psychology	Basic instructional design, educational technology
Adam	Male	White	Instructional designer and technology specialist	M.S.: instructional technology	Advanced instructional design, eLearning, QM
Sally	Female	White	Junior educational technologist	B.A.: computer science	Web-authoring, interactive eLearning, Microsoft suite, LMS expert proficiency
Marge	Female	White	Director, learning design	M.A.: journalism	QM, eLearning, graphic design, expert LMS proficiency
Ted	Male	White	Learning designer specialist	B.A.: communication	Graphic design, basic instructional design
Beth	Female	White	Learning designer specialist	M.A.: art and English	Adobe Creative Cloud advanced instructional design

Theory and Design 43

were White, full-time university employees who interacted directly with faculty and other campus personnel. Table 3.2 presents participant information visually followed by a brief description.

Chloe is the department's senior instructional designer. She has held multiple positions at Lane University ranging from adjunct reading instructor, writing specialist, and now senior instructional designer. ***Chloe*** has a bachelor's degree in English and certifications in training, graphic design, and proficiency levels in D2L and Blackboard LMS.

Paul is the department's instructional designer support. Before joining Lane University three years back, he worked as an entry-level part-time community college instructional designer. ***Paul*** has a bachelor's degree in psychology with certifications in basic instructional design and educational technology.

Adam is the department's instructional designer and technology specialist. He has a master's degree in instructional technology and certifications in advanced instructional design, eLearning, and QM.

Sally is the department's junior educational technologist. Her previous job experience includes a four-year stint as an IT [information technology] personnel at Lane University. She has a bachelor's degree in computer science with multiple certifications in educational technology applications of web-authoring, interactive eLearning, Storyline, Adobe Creative Cloud, and Microsoft suite. She is also certified in LMS expert proficiency levels in D2L, Blackboard, and Canvas.

Marge is the department's learning director and has a total work experience of 16 years. Her job experiences include being a writing specialist and learning designer at Lane University before becoming DE director nine years back. She has a master's degree in journalism and certifications in QM, eLearning, graphic design, and expert proficiency levels in LMS D2L, Blackboard, Moodle, and Canvas.

Ted is a learning designer specialist. His previous job experiences comprise being a studio animator and digital gamer for six years. He has a bachelor's degree in communication with certifications in graphic design and basic instructional design.

Beth is the department's learning designer specialist. Her previous job includes a stint of two years as a part-time contractual learning designer at Lane University. She has a master's degree in art and English and is currently pursuing certifications in Adobe Creative Cloud and advanced instructional design.

End College

I interviewed five participants and analyzed corresponding job descriptions. Out of the five participants interviewed, three were female, while two were male. Three participants were Black, while one was White, and the other

Table 3.3 End College Participants

Pseudonym	Gender	Race	Job Title	Education	Certifications
Carla	Female	Black	Associate director, learning and instructional design	M.A.: curriculum development MBA	Six Sigma, QM, workforce development, LMS proficiency level
Sid	Male	White	Learning designer	B.A.: instructional design	QM, Camtasia, Captivate, LMS proficiency expert levels
Liz	Female	Black	Learning designer	M.A.: education	Project management, instructional design, eLearning
Tina	Female	Black	Director, academic technologies	M.S.: instructional technology B.A.: instructional design	Graphic design, eLearning, Six Sigma, project management, LMS expert levels
Jay	Male	Asian	Instructional design and technology coordinator	B.S.: information technology M.A.: educational technology	eLearning, Adobe Creative Suite, instructional design, LMS expert levels

identified as Asian. All participants were full-time university employees who interacted directly with learners, faculty, and other campus staff. Table 3.3 provides participant information followed by a brief description.

Carla is the OL department's associate director of learning and instructional design. Her diverse job experiences include junior instructional designer and learning designer. She has master's degrees in curriculum development and business administration. **Carla** has multiple certifications in Six Sigma training, QM, workforce development, and LMS proficiency certification in Moodle.

Sid is a learning designer. **Sid** has a bachelor's degree in instructional design. He has certifications in QM, Camtasia, Captivate, and LMS proficiency expert levels in Moodle, Canvas, and WebEx.

Liz is the department's learning designer. She has a master's degree in education with certifications in project management, instructional design, and eLearning.

Tina is the director of academic technologies. She has a master's degree in instructional technology and a bachelor's degree in instructional design. She has certifications in graphic design, eLearning, Six Sigma, project management, LMS expert levels of Moodle, D2L, Sakai, and Canvas.

Jay is the instructional design and technology coordinator. *Jay* has a bachelor's degree in information technology and is currently pursuing a master's degree in educational technology. He has certifications in eLearning, Adobe Creative Suite, instructional design, and LMS expert levels in Moodle and Blackboard.

Data Collection and Analysis

The data collection process entailed getting access to the three sites, getting permission and approval from the human resources (HR) department for requisite job descriptions. Please note that the HR departments at the three sites released the job descriptions on the caveat that they would not be shared, copied, and published. Gathering and analyzing the job descriptions constituted one of my research methods, i.e., content document analysis. Reading through the job descriptions enabled me to select a final participant sample of 17 instructional designers. These 17 instructional designers were interviewed for 45 minutes each, and their job descriptions were analyzed. After all relevant data had been collected, I now proceeded to analyze it.

Data analysis literally means pulling things apart to examine them in their smallest components. It is deconstructing recorded responses to make sense of them, view them through the theoretical lens, and piece the deconstructed responses together in a meaningful way (Lapan et al., 2012). I gathered and analyzed two sets of related data: (a) 17 job descriptions and (b) interview data from 17 interviews, as per my research methodology of basic qualitative design. I did a content analysis of the job descriptions which comprised cyclical stages of reading and developing one- to three-word descriptors for coding.

I also conducted a thorough interview analysis following Marshall and Rossman's (2016) seven-step process of "*organizing the data, immersion in the data, generating categories and themes, coding the data, offering interpretations through analytic memos, searching for alternative understanding, and writing the report*" (p. 217). The analysis was done for three data sets from the three interview sites, i.e., River University, Lane University, and End College. Both content and interview analyses were combined to develop common themes parallel to my research themes of (a) meaning, roles, and function of instructional designers, (b) SLB, and (c) organizational contribution through the theoretical lens of SLB theory.

Conclusion

The lens of SLB combined with my qualitative research methodology provided the base needed to conduct my research investigation. However, before embarking on the investigation, I had to ensure the ethical nature of my study. Research ethics are guidelines and standards that ensure that validity, integrity, and reliability of research are maintained, specifically in the way data is collected, analyzed, and interpreted (Merriam & Tisdell, 2016; Patton, 2015; Yin, 2016). Ensuring research ethics is a two-fold process involving personal ethical research obligations of researcher and ethical standards toward study participants. I fulfilled all ethical requisites and began my study which yielded some surprising results. Ensuing chapters explore and discuss the study's findings and themes.

References

Acevedo, M. M., & Roque, G. (2019). Resisting the deprofessionalization of instructional design. In Y. Vovides & L. R. Lemus (Eds.), Optimizing Instructional Design Methods in Higher Education (pp. 9–26). IGI Global. https://doi.org/10.4018/978-1-5225-4975-8.ch002

Alexander, B., Ashford-Rowe, K., Barajas-Murph, N., Dobbin, G., Knott, J., McCormack, M., Pomerantz, J., Seilhamer, R., & Weber, N. (2019). EDUCAUSE Horizon report 2019. New Media Consortium. https://linhadeleitura.files.wordpress.com/2019/05/2019horizonreport.pdf

Annells, M. (2006). Triangulation of qualitative approaches: Hermeneutical phenomenology and grounded theory. *Journal of Advanced Nursing, 56*(1), 55–61. https://doi.org/10.1111/j.1365-2648.2006.03979.x

Bachman, S. S., Wachman, M., Manning, L., Cohen, A. M., Seifert, R. W., Jones, D. K., Fitzgerald, T., Nuzum, R., & Riley, P. (2017). Social work's role in Medicaid reform: A qualitative study. *American Journal of Public Health, 107*(S3), S250–S255. https://doi.org/10.2105/AJPH.2017.304002

Bond, J., & Dirkin, K. (2018). Instructional design: Study of a widening scope of practice. *Online Journal of Distance Learning Administration, 21*(4), n4.

Brodkin, E. Z. (2011). Policy work: Street-level organizations under new managerialism. *Journal of Public Administration Research and Theory, 21*(suppl_2), i253–i277. https://doi.org/10.1093/jopart/muq093

Caelli, K., Ray, L., & Mill, J. (2003). "Clear as mud": Toward greater clarity in generic qualitative research. *International Journal of Qualitative Methods, 2*(2), 1–24. https://doi.org/10.1177/160940690300200201

Cooper, M. J., Sornalingam, S., & O'Donnell, C. (2015). Street-level bureaucracy: An underused theoretical model for general practice? *British Journal of General Practice, 65*(636), 376–377. 10.3399/bjgp15X685921

Cope, D. G. (2014). Methods and meanings: Credibility and trustworthiness of qualitative research. *Oncology Nursing Forum, 14*(1), 89–91. https://doi.org/10.1188/14.ONF.89-91

Cousin, G. (2010). Positioning positionality. In M. Savin-Baden & C. H. Major (Eds.), *New approaches to qualitative research: Wisdom and uncertainty*, Routledge. (pp. 9–18).

Creswell, J. W. (2013). *Qualitative inquiry and research design: Choosing among five approaches* (3rd ed.). Sage Publishing.

Creswell, J. W., & Creswell, J. D. (2018). *Research design: Qualitative, quantitative, and mixed methods approaches* (5th ed.). SAGE Publications, Inc.

Davidovitz, M., & Cohen, N. (2022). Playing defence: The impact of trust on the coping mechanisms of street-level bureaucrats. *Public Management Review*, *24*(2), 279–300. https://doi.org/10.1080/14719037.2020.1817532

Denzin, N., & Lincoln, Y. (2011). Introduction: The discipline and practice of qualitative research. In N. Denzin & Y. Lincoln (Eds.), *The SAGE handbook of qualitative research* (pp. 1–20). SAGE.

Destler, K. N. (2017). A matter of trust: Street level bureaucrats, organizational climate and performance management reform. *Journal of Public Administration Research and Theory*, *27*(3), 517–534. https://doi.org/10.1093/jopart/muw055

Evans, T. (2010). Professionals, managers and discretion: Critiquing street-level bureaucracy. *The British Journal of Social Work*, *41*(2), 368–386. https://doi.org/10.1093/bjsw/bcq074

Evans, T., & Harris, J. (2004). Street-level bureaucracy, social work and the (exaggerated) death of discretion. *The British Journal of Social Work*, *34*(6), 871–895. https://doi.org/10.1093/bjsw/bch106

Fisher, C. D. (1986). Organizational socialization: An integrative review. In K. M. Rowland & G. R. Ferris (Eds.), *Research in Personnel and Human Resources Management* (Vol. 4, pp. 101–145). JAI Press.

Frisch Aviram, N., Beeri, I., & Cohen, N. (2021). From the bottom-up: Probing the gap between street-level Bureaucrats' intentions of engaging in policy entrepreneurship and their behavior. *The American Review of Public Administration*, *51*(8), 636–649. https://doi.org/10.1177/02750740211023597

Gofen, A. (2014). Mind the gap: Dimensions and influence of street-level divergence. *Journal of Public Administration Research and Theory*, *24*(2), 473–493. https://doi.org/10.1093/jopart/mut037

Howard, F. (2017). *Undocumented students in higher education: A case study exploring street-level bureaucracy in academic advising* [Doctoral dissertation, Virginia Commonwealth University]. VCU theses and dissertations. https://doi.org/10.25772/1A6T-BP55

Hupe, P., & Hill, M. (2007). Street-Level bureaucracy and public accountability. *Public Administration*, *85*(2), 279–299. https://doi.org/10.1111/j.1467-9299.2007.00650.x

Jones, C. (2001). Voices from the front line: State social workers and New Labour. British Journal of Social Work, 31(4), 547–562. https://doi.org/10.1093/bjsw/31.4.547

Kahlke, R. M. (2014). Generic qualitative approaches: Pitfalls and benefits of methodological mixology. International journal of qualitative methods, 13(1), 37–52. https://doi.org/10.1177/160940691401300119

Keiser, L. R. (2010). Understanding street-level bureaucrats' decision making: Determining eligibility in the social security disability program. *Public Administration Review*, *70*(2), 247–257. https://doi.org/10.1111/j.1540-6210.2010.02131.x

Korstjens, I., & Moser, A. (2018). Series: Practical guidance to qualitative research. Part 4: Trustworthiness and publishing. *European Journal of General Practice*, *24*(1), 120–124. https://doi.org/10.1080/13814788.2017.1375092

Krefting, L. (1991). Rigor in qualitative research: The assessment of trustworthiness. *American Journal of Occupational Therapy*, *45*(3), 214–222. https://doi.org/10.5014/ajot.45.3.214

Lapan, S. D., Quartaroli, M. T., & Riemer, F. J. (2012). *Qualitative research: An introduction to methods and designs*. Jossey-Bass.

Larson, M. B., & Lockee, B. B. (2004). Instructional design practice: Career environments, job roles, and a climate of change. *Performance Improvement Quarterly* 17(1), 22–40. https://doi.org/10.1111/j.1937-8327.2004.tb00300.x

Lincoln, E. G., & Guba, Y. S. (1985). *Naturalistic inquiry*. Sage.

Lipsky, M. (1980). *Street-level bureaucracy: Dilemmas of the individual in public services*. Russel Sage Foundation.

Lipsky, M. (2010). *Street-level bureaucracy: Dilemmas of the individual in public service*. Russell Sage Foundation.

Loyens, K., & Maesschalck, J. (2010). Toward a theoretical framework for ethical decision making of street-level bureaucracy: Existing models reconsidered. *Administration & Society*, 42(1), 66–100. https://doi.org/10.1177/0095399710362524

Magnusson, D. (1981). *Situational determinants of stress: An interactional perspective*. University of Stockholm.

Mann, S. (2011). *The research interview: Reflective practice and reflexivity in research processes*. Palgrave Macmillan. https://doi.org/10.1057/9781137353368

Marshall, C., & Rossman, G. B. (2016). *Designing qualitative research*. Sage Publications, Inc. https://doi.org/10.4236/psych.2013.411A005

Maynard-Moody, S. W., Musheno, M., & Musheno, M. C. (2003). *Cops, teachers, counselors: Stories from the front lines of public service*. University of Michigan Press.

Merriam, S. B., & Tisdell, E. J. (2015). *Qualitative research: A guide to design and implementation* (4th ed.). Jossey-Bass.

Merriam, S. B., & Tisdell, E. J. (2016). *Qualitative research: A guide to design and implementation*. John Wiley & Sons.

Moore, S. T. (1987). The theory of street-level bureaucracy: A positive critique. *Administration & Society*, 19(1), 74–94. https://doi.org/10.1177/009539978701900104

Patton, M. Q. (2015). *Qualitative research and methods: Integrating theory and practice*. Sage Publications.

Shenton, A. K. (2004). Strategies for ensuring trustworthiness in qualitative research projects. *Education for Information*, 22(2), 63–75. https://doi.org/10.3233/EFI-2004-22201

Surry, D. W., & Robinson, M. A. (2001). A taxonomy of instructional technology service positions in higher education. *Innovations in Education and Teaching International*, 38(3), 231–238. https://doi.org/10.1080/14703290110051406

Tracy, S. J. (2019). *Qualitative research methods: Collecting evidence, crafting analysis, communicating impact*. John Wiley & Sons.

Yin, R. K. (2016). *Qualitative research from start to finish* (2nd ed.). The Guilford Press.

4 Instructional Designer Perceptions vs Official Job Descriptions

The first theme of researching instructional designer perceptions about their work, their roles, their functions, and their identity was explored at the three higher educational institutions of River University, Lane University, and End College. Requisite job descriptions were analyzed, and corresponding participants were interviewed. This theme is discussed in two parts: (a) defining instructional design and (b) job roles and functions. This section will unpack these questions: do institutional job descriptions and instructional designer perceptions have the same definition of instructional design? Is it different and how? Is there an alignment or mismatch between job descriptions and instructional designer perceptions?

River University

There was a mismatch of instructional design definition between university job descriptions and instructional designer perceptions. Instructional design was ADDIE (analysis, design, development, evaluation, implementation of instruction) which was a singular complete definition. This was evident in job description references of *"educational design and development, program evaluation and implementation, learner analysis and technology integration."*

However, participants believed that the definition of instructional design was not ADDIE. The definition of instructional design was dependent on the individual, that is, how they saw and perceived instructional design, their job role and function. **Ann** defined it as course design with functions of developing curriculum flows, storyboards, content organization such as chunking and sequencing content into weekly instruction, and accessibility checks. She said, *"Instructional design cannot be defined as one. It means different things to different people."* Defending her view, **Ann** said that being the instructional design and access (IDA) director, she saw instructional design as the method of course design. To others instructional design would mean something else. **Ellie**, the learning management system (LMS) specialist, defined instructional design as LMS Blackboard with functions of *"uploading courses*

DOI: 10.4324/9781003426806-4

to Blackboard, fixing Blackboard glitches" which is consistent with her job responsibilities.

Roles and Functions

There was an alignment between roles and functions as stated on university job descriptions and instructional designer perceptions of those roles and functions. According to official job descriptions and instructional designer perceptions, instructional designers performed two types of overlapping roles: (a) relationship building and (b) support. University job descriptions spoke of relationship building specifically as functions of being faculty and student liaison, project management, and informal leadership. These functions were viewed as the foundation for support functions of training, educational technology, and course design. Job description references such as *"being part of a team, collaborating and consulting, effectively interact"* emphasized the necessity of having working relations to perform support functions of *"Blackboard training, completing projects on time."*

Relation-Building Functions

Participants agreed that the three relationship-building functions were dependent on having positive working relations with different campus personnel. **Ann** said, *"how we deal with different people, develop working relations of open communication, trust, and respect I think gives us the chance to do other tasks and provide support."* Working relations were considered the stepping-stone to providing support and assistance to campus staff. Positive working relations were characterized by teamwork, communication, collaboration, and influence.

PROJECT MANAGEMENT

The relationship-building function of project management, according to participants, was the key to understanding other functions and tasks of training, educational technology, faculty and student liaison, course design, and informal leadership. **Ann** said, *"Projects involve all our functions like projects on web accessibility training, LMS projects on Blackboard updates and interactive e-learning. Projects I think are the base and lead to everything."* Sharing her own experience of working on an educational technology project of putting employee-onboarding systems on social media platforms Facebook and Twitter, she said, *"it was just one project, but it led to other functions."* These other functions included training the Human Resources (HR) department about the social media platform, mentoring, and overseeing what the trainees were doing, coaching them about how to design the system for uploading onto the app, working with HR to write and format the content for the system, and uploading the system on the app.

Successful project work depended on having positive working relations of open communication, trust, respect, and understanding with campus personnel. ***Ann*** believed that positive working relations led to influence, participation, and open discussion, and subsequent successful completion of the project in scheduled time. ***Nan*** said, "*When you work on a project with different people, you talk, discuss and develop a working relation.*" Having working relations enabled IDA members to voice their opinion, question, argue, suggest, and influence other people. To ***Bess***, a working relationship meant working with diverse people, listening, and adjusting personal views for the achievement of a common goal. To quote ***Bess***, "*It's about working together not as individuals with our own goals and biases but working and discussing together to develop online courses or solve an LMS issue achieving a goal together.*"

FACULTY AND STUDENT LIAISON

A primary relationship-building function was being a student and faculty liaison. For ***Ellie***, ***Ann***, and ***Kirk***, being a faculty and student liaison was about communication and collaboration. ***Ellie*** said that being a student and faculty liaison involved "*timely communication where students and faculty understood each other's expectations.*" ***Kirk*** saw it as a medium for ensuring that students knew about faculty standards and expectations and vice versa. Liaisons tried to close the gap between students and faculty by, as ***Kirk*** put it, "*getting them on the same page*" where they knew and understood each other's expectations and demands. ***Ann*** added another caveat of parent involvement to the liaison function. She said, "*I think a liaison works to inform and educate parents, like parents of new students who are joining or transferring.*" A liaison communicated and worked with other departments such as orientation, advising, and financial aid to ensure parents understood and were aware of university vision, college protocols, and financial aid procedures. The liaison function depended on tasks of communication, interactions, and as described in the job descriptions "*excellent presentation skills.*"

INFORMAL LEADERSHIP

Informal leadership was about communication, influence, and not being an authoritative figure giving instructions. To ***Ann*** and ***Nan*** informal leadership was making people aware of the current situation, suggesting options, persuading, and influencing them to adopt changes. ***Nan*** believed that informal leaders worked through collaboration, which she described as "*working with different people, respecting their knowledge and skill and gaining their trust* *for a cause."* She shared experiences of being a *"frequent flyer"* or working with HR to streamline employee onboarding systems, working with faculty and IT to write quality courses for students and embed them online with interactive cloud technology. While to **Ann**, informal leadership was developing a *"network of communication, and teamwork."* She felt that every IDA member was an informal leader who worked with faculty, staff, and students and established positive working relationships. These working relations, she emphasized, gave IDA the confidence *"to discuss, argue, question, persuade and influence others"* to recognize and acknowledge faulty and obsolete systems and policies.

Support Functions

Participants believed that the support functions of training, educational technology, and course design developed from relationship-building functions. **Kirk** said, *"the support we give comes from our working relations. I mean if we have good working relations-trust, respect, teamwork, and all that. Giving support becomes easy."* For instance, embedding educational technology apps or troubleshooting LMS glitches was dependent on how smoothly IDA members collaborated and communicated with campus staff to adopt suggested improvements.

TRAINING

Training was viewed as being dependent on and influenced by the relationship-building function of being faculty and student liaison. **Ann** described training as, *"kind of formal student and faculty liaison. We formally sit in a training room, lecture, PowerPoints and practice but essentially it is mentoring and coaching."* Training was a forum of active listening and working with diverse people together, encouraging an open dialogue, and suggesting improvements and changes. **Bess** elaborated, *"when we train, we discuss and learn new stuff, share and ask questions and create. Have new ideas and all this helps."* In fact, **Kirk** said that IDA's primary job function was that of training, *"lending support and discussing latest knowledge, technology, rubrics."* These views suggest that training is dependent on open communication, sharing, and an exchange of ideas.

EDUCATIONAL TECHNOLOGY

Participants agreed that the educational technology function which included LMS tasks was heavily influenced by the relationship-building function of project management. To **Bess** and **Kirk**, the educational technology comprised working on projects of Blackboard (LMS) integrations such as seamlessly incorporating video, cloud, web, and social learning tools on the LMS. It involved working with different departments, informing, and sharing the Blackboard integrations, usages, and advantages. To quote **Kirk**, "*It's mainly about telling people what ed tech is out there, what suits us and how to use it.*" For example, integrating the Kaltura cloud video technology in Blackboard to develop and share videos and other interactive media content in biology undergraduate courses. "*I had to study Kaltura, know why it is used, and can it be used for our courses, will learners and even faculty use it, ease of access, so many things to think of,*" **Kirk** ended smiling. To **Ellie** and **Nan**, the educational technology function meant uploading, migrating, and checking functionality of courses which were *live* or being used for that semester.

COURSE DESIGN

Participants agreed that defining course design as a separate support function was hard. **Bess**, **Nan**, and **Ellie** described course design as tasks of writing and formatting instruction into weekly modules as a "*kind of training, being liaison.*" **Ellie** said, "*writing content into instruction depends on training and mentoring everyone on quality writing, web guidelines and stuff.*" **Ellie** believed that course design tasks of writing, editing, formatting such as chunking and sequencing the instruction into weekly modules for LMS were dependent on other support tasks and functions of training, mentoring, discussion, and researching.

To **Kirk** and **Ann** course design also included educational technology and LMS functions. **Ann** described course design as an "*umbrella support function*" which encompassed all support functions and tasks. She said, "*training, inputting audio and video apps, coaching, everything comes under course design.*" She referred to her experience of designing courses for the Math department. "*My role was that of writing and formatting, but that single function required discussing, ed tech, LMS, training, you know. It's like course design means all functions.*"

New Roles

Relationship-building functions of project management, informal leadership, and faculty and student liaison were viewed as harbinger of new roles of being strategic partners and social agents. Participants viewed themselves as *strategic partners* of course design and college protocols of LMS Blackboard standards, web accessibility guidelines, and college vision and goals. **Kirk** said, "*We work with executive leadership, deans and all to set standards, a uniform standard about how courses should be, what is our instruction going to be like.*" To **Ann**, being a strategic partner was about collaborating with campus leadership to "*disseminate, advocate, streamline*" systems and processes. It involved partnering to improve university systems and policies, remove outdated protocols, and keep the university systems current.

The role of strategic partner was viewed as a launch-pad for the instructional design role of *social agent*. **Ann** believed that IDA personnel acted as social agents on campus who developed an open forum of dialogue and exchange of ideas. The forum according to **Bess** allowed all campus employees to freely express opinions about campus operations. *"We discuss, share, and develop new methods, new standards. It's like discussing to do better stuff,"* she said. **Nan** felt that the forum initiated social change at the grassroot level of employee groups. *"It makes us aware of what is missing, how things should be like not working beyond the specified time, average salaries for our positions in the state and it all helps in having informed employees."* Such remarks indicate that the social agency role meant being an informed employee who engaged in open and participative communication to develop new methods and ideas.

Lane University

Lane University's formal definition of instructional design aligned with instructional designer perceptions of instructional design. Both defined instructional design as the process of developing instruction in all three formats of face to face, online, and hybrid. Instructional design, according to university job descriptions, was viewed as a combination of *"analysis, development, and implementation, prepare courses, writing and editing courses, program and course design, computer based and multimedia applications"* functions and tasks which enabled instructional development.

Participant responses were two connected overlapping perspectives on the same theme. Both perspectives defined instructional design as a course design process, but in different ways. The first perspective was that the instructional design definition was dependent on the person developing the instruction, that is, their official job role and function. **Marge**, **Chloe**, **Ted**, and **Beth** defined instructional design as a course design process. **Marge** said, *"I think it is all the functions of designing courses whether for LMS or face to face."* She spoke about course design functions of learner needs analyses, surveys, interviews, background checks, quality writing, research, storyboarding, compliance, and content organization activities of chunking and sequencing of content into weekly instruction.

The second perspective was put forth by educational technologists such as **Adam** and **Sally** who defined instructional design as functions of educational technology. To them, definition of instructional design depended on the user/learner of the instruction. How the learner viewed and used instructional design shaped its method and purpose. **Adam** explained, *"it depends on learners, like most of them are adult working people and they like to learn at their* *own pace.*" Adult working learners, according to ***Adam***, preferred "*learning on the go at their own convenience*" rather than static classroom learning and "*so I think ed tech methods which put instruction online, virtual is instructional design.*" These methods included using social and eLearning apps, interactive games, and MOOC (massive open online courses). Likewise, ***Sally*** believed it was not possible to embed educational technology apps, links, or eLearning segments without writing and formatting the course. She said, "*Ed tech I think is a part of course design. eLearning and stuff make the design more easy, attractive, and accessible. We call it enhancing the course. That's what ed. tech does.*" Course design therefore involved instructional writing and formatting, and then embedding appropriate educational technology in the instruction to make it accessible for all learners.

Roles and Functions

Instructional designer job roles and functions partially aligned between university job descriptions and instructional designer perceptions. The instructional designer supports the job role with functions of educational technology, LMS, training, design and development, and project management given in job descriptions aligned with instructional designer perceptions of their roles and functions. However, distance education (DE) instructional designers also stated they performed a responsive job role with functions of student and faculty liaison, and informal leadership not mentioned in official job descriptions.

Support Roles

Official job descriptions spoke about instructional designers as "*project managers who trained, designed integrated technology, streamlined, and provided support.*" The support functions of project management, educational technology, training, and course design are described below.

PROJECT MANAGEMENT

Project management was viewed as an umbrella function with activities of educational technology, LMS, training, and course design. This was because as ***Marge*** said, "*We have different projects and each project deals with different issues like training projects or LMS projects.*" Similarly, ***Beth*** and ***Adam*** felt that, irrespective of official designations, all DE personnel worked on projects. ***Beth*** said, "*our participation may differ like I am usually this writing guy who just follows instructions.*" ***Adam*** agreed that their role on projects determined their level of participation, discussion, and collaboration. He felt that it did not matter what the project was, "*it is LMS, design or compliance*," and his function was fixed and limited to LMS and agreeing to everything.

Remarks of these two participants indicated one-way communication, discussion, and collaboration with limited autonomy to voice suggestions and interact. As **Adam** said, their role was "*merely agreeing and nodding along to everything decided by higher ups.*"

This perspective of the DE project role as lacking importance and relevance was further validated by **Paul** who described the project role of DE personnel as "*silent sleeping staff*" who do tasks without questioning their relevance and importance. **Paul's** observation indicated that instructional designers were not involved in project operation, nor did they actively communicate and collaborate. The roles of instructional designers were limited to writing, proofreading, and LMS troubleshooting. **Paul** described these roles as minor and inconsequential as they could be done by anyone and "*did not require instructional design knowledge and skill.*" These views suggest a narrow outlook where instructional designers received and followed directives and instructions from faculty and executive leaders such as directors and deans.

TRAINING

The support function of training was viewed as an extension of the educational technology and LMS activities of D2L enrollment and registration, navigation, participation, and educational technology apps of using and linking virtual classrooms. Other training included lectures on LMS accessibility and compliance standards, course writing, and editing. **Sally** and **Chloe** believed that the DE personnel were involved in training related to their job designation. For example, **Sally**, who was an educational technologist, said she always did educational technology and LMS training. She clarified,

> See, I train everyone here—faculty, staff and sometimes students about D2L, uploading interactive apps into D2L, downloading activities, uploading final grades, putting in OER [online educational resources] links—I am an ed. tech. trainer.

The narrow scope of training was further explained by **Beth**, **Marge**, and **Adam** who stated that training topics and schedule were pre-decided. Training topics, whether LMS, instructional writing, or LMS, said **Adam**, were determined by executive leaders and not decided by faculty, staff, students, or the DE department. **Beth** said, "*We just follow what is set, usually it is ed. tech and LMS training first and then course design such as writing.*" Such views hint at a top-down channel of communication, comparable to participant perspectives regarding a closed one-way channel of receiving and following instructions from executive leaders while performing project management and training tasks.

COURSE DESIGN

Job descriptions defined course design function as tasks of developing curriculum flows, storyboarding, content writing, and organizational tasks of chunking and sequencing the content into weekly instruction. However, **Chloe** dismissed this multi-faceted course design function when she said, *"What we do is nothing fancy as design and development."* **Chloe** explained that course design at Lane University meant following instructions to write course content, editing, and checking for grammar and spelling mistakes. *"Like in Business College—take the written instruction and proofread it."* Her comment indicated the description of course design in university job descriptions was different from that of instructional designer views. **Ted**, **Marge**, and **Beth** seconded this view that the meaning of course design was narrow and limited to writing and researching subject content. **Ted** complained that he was not involved in any course design functions of developing storyboards and doing compliance checks but *"just do content writing and proofreading. Here I have become a writer and proofreader."*

Contrary to official job descriptions, DE participants stated that course design comprised educational technology and LMS tasks of embedding, developing, and producing educational technology apps, social and mobile learning links, eLearning games, D2L (LMS) navigation, and course uploading. **Adam** said that it was not feasible or possible to research and embed educational technology apps, links, 3D virtual eLearning without having the written weekly content. **Sally** felt the same and said, *"We need the weekly content to do educational technology and stuff. We cannot embed ed tech without knowing the course content, its objectives, and weekly topics."* The knowledge enabled them to understand what educational technology and eLearning app could benefit the course and make it attractive and learner-oriented. These remarks coincide with the definition of instructional design previously put forth by these two educational technologists as dependent on individual job role and function. Consequently, the views of these two participants focus on importance, relevance, and the critical role of educational technology tasks in course design. Overall, participant views indicate the centrality of course design function and corresponding tasks to the design and development of instruction.

Responsive Role

The responsive role was not listed in university job descriptions but was performed by DE instructional designers. The rationale for this role, as explained by **Marge**, was that it was not possible to fulfill and resolve all clients and campus issues by only doing stated official functions. DE instructional designers had to go beyond and bend established rules, systems, and norms to meet and satisfy diverse client issues. She said, *"Sometimes just training* or writing a course just doesn't cut it. Faculty or staff or even learners and maybe even deans want something more and we have to give that something more." Along with **Chloe** and **Adam**, **Marge** argued, "*this act and function of doing something more, responding to different needs, expectations, problems is something we do on our own.*" These responsive functions of going beyond official functions included being student and faculty liaison, and informal grassroot leaders.

FACULTY AND STUDENT LIAISON

A primary responsive function at Lane University was being a faculty and student liaison. To **Ted**, **Beth**, and **Paul**, this meant coaching, mentoring, advising, and helping people understand and accomplish their goals. **Paul** described the liaison function as bending and adjusting established training norms and formats to "*hand holding*" and constantly "*being on their side.*" **Beth** described the liaison function as that of being a resource library on various instructional design methods. She said, "*they [faculty, staff, students] see me as a library you know have all the answers about D2L, storyboards, learning models and stuff.*" Being a resource library helped her provide one-to-one advice to students on "*fixing D2L glitches, uploading assignments, and projects.*" To **Ted**, the liaison function guided and informed faculty about course writing protocols, web accessibility guidelines, instructional design models, virtual classroom activities, and how to chunk and sequence content into weekly instruction.

Being the liaison also meant promotion of the DE department's services. **Marge** believed that being a student and faculty was informing, educating, and promoting the different services of the DE department. In her words the liaison function was "*building visibility for our services and all options.*" **Chloe** stated that the liaison task was to "*create awareness about what DE does and what it can do, how it can help.*" She said that the goal of being the liaison was to ensure that campus personnel, whether it was faculty, staff, or students, understood each other's purpose and function—"*bringing everyone together.*" These views indicate open participation and communication, contrary to prior views about a closed one-way system of receiving instructions and not voicing suggestions while performing project management and training functions.

INFORMAL LEADERSHIP

Another responsive function was that of informal grassroot leadership. Participants agreed that grassroot leaders cut across department formal hierarchies and established an open forum for discussion, reflection, and participation. To **Chloe** and **Marge**, being grassroot leaders was being proactive and actively listening and suggesting options. **Chloe** said, "*try to solve problems—taking* *the initiative and trying to fix things."* Supported by her colleagues, ***Chloe*** believed that as informal grassroot leaders, instructional designers did not wait for problems to happen. They anticipated and developed ways to solve issues at departmental levels. This indicates a reliance on personality attributes to work as responsive grassroot leaders and practice street-level divergence. Yet, at the same time these views appear contrary to previous participant arguments about limited communication of only receiving instructions and not discussing or exchanging information and ideas in functions of project management and training.

End College

College job descriptions defined instructional design as the design process of instruction. Indeed, college job description references such as *"course design and development of all educational technology projects, analyze and apply instructional design theories, practices and methods, selecting appropriate educational technology and identifying course delivery strategies"* revealed a focus on the methods/process of design.

Participant responses were divided into two perspectives. The first perspective held by ***Liz***, ***Tina***, and ***Sid*** believed that instructional design did not have a singular definition. It comprised two sequential related parts, that is, the foundational learning theories which lead to the design of instruction. ***Liz*** said,

> *Methods of design and development are always changing like new ed. tech, new eLearning, interactive storyboards. This is the changing part of instructional design but the foundation, the science part of learning design seldom changes.*

Liz shared an example of writing instruction for STEM (science, technology, engineering, and mathematics) classes that were based on the neurocognitive learning theory of connectivism. The theory never changed, but the design method ranged on a continuum from eLearning to games or avatars. ***Sid*** explained it with an equation, *"theory + process=instructional design."* He said that when developing courses, instructional designers used learning theories as the *"base to launch design methods."* ***Tina*** shared that learning theories shaped design of instruction. She said, *"Be it social learning, constructivism, or cognitive. They all influence how we write instruction, the course goals, weekly objectives."* Such views suggest the important influence of learning theories in determining design, method, and purpose of instruction.

The second perspective held by ***Jay*** and ***Carla*** spoke about the influences that shaped the design of instruction. ***Jay*** believed learners determined what and how the instruction was going to be designed. Designing courses for adult learners was different from designing courses for traditional on campus students. Adult students preferred courses with educational technology links, apps, interactive videos, and podcasts. *Jay* said, "*Adult students want courses which have lots of ed tech., on social apps of Facebook, OERs which link to interactive web videos and e-learning.*" Whereas traditional on campus students wanted courses with basic Moodle (LMS) apps such as Moodle docs and weekly discussion forums. *Carla* believed that course content and goal were influenced by faculty expectations. She said, "*It's like every instructor has her own standards and course goals, like what they want from students in that course.*" She paused and said slowly, "*That is why each course is designed differently [laughing] not one course design for all.*" Such views suggest that designs are different for each course depending on learner and faculty needs and expectations.

Roles and Functions

There was an alignment between job roles and functions in college job descriptions and instructional designer perceptions. Instructional designers were viewed as supportive staff with functions of course design, training, educational technology, LMS, project management, leadership, and faculty and student liaison. The centrality of the instructional designer support role was evident in references from job descriptions, "*support education technology needs, point of contact, design, promote and deliver innovative activities and workshops, provide leadership, supports the planning, designing, and development of effective online and hybrid learning experiences, communicate and collaborate with faculty or subject matter experts.*" Participants agreed with the same.

Project Management

This supportive function was viewed by all participants as the foundation which led to other support functions. For instance, the function of project management had participants working in teams on different projects of training, LMS, content writing, compliance, and educational technology. To *Carla* working on projects meant working with diverse people, adjusting, and respecting their knowledge and skills to establish a working rapport. She said, "*Like compliance projects, some of us are instructional designers and know what it is but guys from IT, and some teaching folks don't know, and we have to understand and work with them.*" Her comment indicated the importance of building good working relations with campus personnel to enable smooth and effective interaction, collaboration, and exchange of information. Online learning (OL) instructional designers, *Carla* reflected, were heavily invested in developing positive working relations to successfully complete projects at the scheduled time.

Project work involved working with people, discussing, sharing, arguing, and understanding each other's view to reach a solution. Sometimes, *Tina* said, "*we give in and accept the other person's view. We push aside our ego and pride and interacting, communicating, dividing work*" to accomplish the project goal. A positive working relation involved working with team members to make them realize, acknowledge, and reach a satisfying conclusion. To *Sid*, project management meant acknowledging and respecting each other as "*professionals*" who worked and interacted to accomplish a goal.

Course Design

OL participants viewed course design as a dominant supportive function. The course design function comprised tasks of writing, editing, research, analysis, compliance, formatting of content into weekly instruction, that is, chunking and sequencing, and accessibility checks of online, hybrid, and face-to-face courses. *Liz* explained, "*We have a system like face-to-face for our campus students, some hybrid also, and most online and hybrid stuff for our adult students, workforce.*" Design and development functions meant being knowledgeable about storyboarding, creating curriculum workflows to show the process of design and responsibilities of each person. These flows directed design and development efforts such as how to work with subject-matter experts (SME), what, why, when, and how to write.

The analysis task of course design comprised investigating learner and faculty needs and expectations through tasks of background checks, surveys, and individual interviews. *Jay*, *Tina*, and *Carla*, all spoke of the importance and relevance of this course design task. According to *Tina* and *Carla*, shared analysis tasks comprised learner and faculty analysis. *Tina* described both analysis tasks as "*the foundation which influences how instruction is written, what design is used.*" *Jay* noted that a comprehensive and accurate learner needs analysis "*streamlines everything, showing where to focus on, like which learner needs and demands, you know, when we write instruction.*" *Carla* spoke about how faculty analysis led to developing weekly or session instructional courses from subject content. Faculty analysis, she said, was finding out "*instructor expectations, standards and demands to write the content in weekly instruction.*" It determined which educational technology to use and how. Doing both learner and faculty analysis before developing and designing instruction ensured smooth and effective instructional design. In fact, the views of these three participants mirrored participant descriptions about learner and faculty influences on instructional design. Course design function appears to be the foundation of instructional design.

Educational Technology

The supportive function of educational technology and LMS was viewed as overlapping with that of course design. *Jay*, *Carla*, and *Liz* viewed all educational technology tasks as a part of course design. As per *Liz* course design analysis tasks *"mean understanding and putting in educational technology standards, apps, and links into all courses."* While *Jay* felt the level and degree of educational technology embedded in a course depended on learner needs and faculty. He said, *"It all goes back to doing a learner needs analysis and finding out if they are comfortable with ed. tech and what kind they want."* Learners, therefore, were the key to understanding, knowing, and embedding educational technology apps such as interactive eLearning, games, avatars, podcasts, OER (open educational resource) links, or social and mobile learning networks of Twitter and Facebook.

The meaning and scope of educational technology also comprised selection and maintenance of educational technology equipment and facilities on campus. *Tina* and *Sid* felt that a relative task of educational technology was to know who needed what technology, in what format, when, and where. *Tina* argued that it was the responsibility of OL instructional designers to *"keep an eye that everything is working well for learners to understand and participate."* Whether it was hybrid, face-to-face, or online classes, OL instructional designers ensured that educational technology equipment of links, videos, podcasts, SMART technology equipment, and virtual gaming equipment were functional. To do so, *Tina* felt it was important to have working relations with campus staff. She said, *"Working relations don't have to be good and friendly, any kind will do. We should just know if something goes wrong and people need our help."* *Sid* agreed a positive or negative working relation *"doesn't matter which kind as long as we have that communication thing going and people know we are there to help with our tech. stuff."* Their views indicated the importance of working relations to secure educational technology help. Overall, educational technology emerged as an encompassing function with a wide scope and ties to course design tasks.

Training

The supportive function of training was viewed by all participants as encompassing all functions and tasks of support. *Carla* and *Liz* spoke about training projects which blended supportive functions of educational technology, LMS, and course design. To quote *Liz*, *"we train on everything, Moodle [LMS] stuff, quality writing rubrics, social learning apps."* Training was described by *Carla* as *"open-ended, flexible, and discussive consulting"* which was dependent on working relations. Training meant an open forum of information, knowledge, skill, and ideas acquisition, exchange, and development. Elaborating further, *Carla* stated, *"our training is not fixed. Topics are always* changing. Usually, learners decide our training topic. Like right now our training is on compliance and WCAG guidelines [web content accessibility guidelines], and LMS integrations."

Along with training topics, even the training method and approach was shaped by the needs and wants of trainees. According to **Tina**, the training method and approach was not pre-decided but depended on what trainees thought they needed. She said, "*We may decide to do a lecture training on Moodle updates but then one of the people doing the training may come up and say, we want a hands-on workshop on Moodle. And so, we have to do it.*" **Sid** reiterated this view that sometimes, training workshops began with lectures and demonstrations of content writing and organization but soon changed to a participative "*round table question and answer*" format. He felt this fluidity in training approach and format was a credit to the open and flexible design of training. He said,

Our training is not fixed [laughing] I kind of see it as a free for all where trainees come, listen, and then may decide hey we know this stuff, or we don't really need a formal lecture on quality writing standards, how about discussing it and doing some practical stuff?

The idea of training being flexible as well as transportable was validated by **Jay**, who talked about how the formal classroom training with lectures and PowerPoints changed into informal personal mentoring, coaching, and advising when "*it goes outside the training room.*" His remark indicated that training was not only dependent on learner needs but also extended beyond the classroom. All these views indicate the wide and fluid scope of the formal training function influenced by learners and sometimes goes beyond formal boundaries to flow into other supportive tasks of mentoring and coaching.

Faculty and Student Liaison

Informal and personal training was described as the supportive function of being a student and faculty liaison. **Tina** argued that being a liaison was "*training students, faculty and sometimes even parents to have the right correct info.*" It involved "*constant interaction, mentoring and handholding*" to ensure that students and faculty understood each other's demands and needs. To **Sid**, the liaison function was being a "*salesperson*" who shared information to promote the college services and vision to new students and parents. It meant being a "*middleman*" who analyzed learner needs and "*so knew what learners wanted in their courses.*" Constant interaction with faculty and staff combined with theoretical and latest knowledge equipped instructional designers to "*bridge the gap between learner needs and faculty expectations.*" His view indicated that being a student and faculty liaison was about an open channel of communication between students, parents, staff, and faculty so that they knew expectations of each other. There was no room for misconceptions and preconceived ideas. These perceptions strongly resonate with participants' prior views describing the liaison function as informal training characterized by open participation, communication, exchange of information, and advocacy of college services.

Informal Leadership

Training branched into the supportive function of informal leadership where OL personnel interacted, influenced, and led project teams through constant communication and influence. To **Carla**, informal leadership was "*supervising, overseeing, and leading people on design issues.*" Informal leadership, like training and the liaison function, involved establishing a channel of positive and open communication. This positive communication was based on respect, understanding, and appreciation for each other's knowledge and skill. **Jay** felt that every OL employee was an informal leader since "*everyone was on a team and could interact and influence.*" Informal leadership, he argued, was "*really being the expert in instructional design to talk, convince others, influence them what to do,*" for example, influencing the Engineering Dean to recommend using the educational technology app Articulate in engineering courses. **Jay** felt that being the expert in educational technology helped as "*it makes people listen and work with you.*" Informal leadership was about open and positive communication where instructional designers, due to their expertise, got opportunities to persuade, influence, and convince campus people.

Persuasive communication which could influence and convince people was viewed as a challenging leadership responsibility. According to **Tina**, informal leadership could become a sensitive issue when OL staff were working with faculty who might resent them and view them as interfering with their classroom. She expressed that OL informal leaders "*have to be careful not to step on other people's toes, be friendly and try to get everyone together.*" She shared her experience of working with a history professor who did not like her approach to developing instruction, using timeline simulations, role plays, and case studies. She and her co-worker had to schedule regular weekly meetings, present curriculum flow charts to help the professor understand that they were, in fact, like him working to improve instruction for his students. Informal leadership, she went on to explain, was not being an authoritative figure and forcing decisions on other people. Agreeing with her colleagues, she felt that informal leadership was "*talking to people, finding common ground, explaining why stuff should be done and what's in it for them?*" Supporting her view, **Liz** said informal leadership involved "*Persuading and showing the other person how doing an activity is going to benefit them, its, what's in it for me?*" **Liz** believed that people tended to listen and follow ideas and rules originally disapproved of by them if they were informed of how they would benefit from them. These views suggest that informal leadership is about establishing open and positive channels of two-way communication to help and find middle ground to reconcile and accommodate diverse opinions.

Analysis and Conclusion

Participants across the three institutions defined instructional design as a design process. River University and Lane University instructional designers saw instructional design as dependent on their job role and function. For instance, educational technologists defined it as educational technology, while learning designers described it as course design. To these River and Lane University instructional designers, instructional design comprised both course design and educational technology functions. These functions included writing, research, editing, content formatting such as chunking and sequencing, compliance, conducting learner and faculty needs analyses, all educational technology tasks, LMS navigation, and troubleshooting. Another commonality was the influences on the design and development of instruction. Both River University and End College instructional designers focused on the importance of learners influencing the content, structure, and design of instruction. However, End College instructional designers also spoke about faculty expectations as influencing instructional method and content. To these instructional designers, the definition of instructional design as a design process was incomplete and inadequate. They focused on the theoretical underpinnings of instructional design, that is, the various learning theories which shaped and influenced how instruction was designed. They believed it was not possible to design instruction without having the foundation of theory to guide them. Instructional design was *theory* + *design* process.

Instructional designer perceptions about the meaning of instructional design were varied and lacked comprehensiveness and singularity. Definitions were one-sided and highlighted a particular skill or influence. This could be because instructional designers lacked holistic knowledge of instructional design as an academic discipline. Their knowledge was processual and skill-based centering on design methods, theories, and influences. It could also be that instruction design as an academic discipline is too broad and ambiguous with many meanings, competencies, and theories which confuse practitioners and academicians.

Another factor is the impact of this ambiguity on the professional identity of instructional designers. How do they view themselves? Do they see themselves according to their job function and role as River University instructional designers? Or do they view their role as related to their clientele such as at End College where the role and definition of instructional design was shaped and influenced by adult and traditional learners?

Job Roles and Functions

Instructional designers relied heavily on their institutional job descriptions to guide their job behavior and performance. Instructional designers used these university job descriptions as reasons for doing their work such as content writing, educational technology, and training. At the same time, they also used these job descriptions to justify doing extra functions or for not doing their work. For example, the official functions of finite resource management, training, and project management in job descriptions were used to justify developing norms of developing working relations.

Findings across the three institutions identified support as a common job role, aligned to the official job role given in job descriptions. Instructional designers, irrespective of team structure and culture or hierarchical structure and closed culture, performed three common support functions of course design, educational technology, and training. This similarity between the three structurally and culturally different higher education institutions suggests that instructional design job role has a common base or foundation of support. Another common function was that of project management which was identified as an *umbrella function* as it launched and developed other functions and tasks such as course design, LMS, training, student and faculty liaison, and informal leadership. All these functions depended on the development of working relations which enabled these instructional designers to share, discuss, and exchange information and ideas. In fact, working relations were the bedrock which led to open communication and interaction and thus led to successful and smooth completion of all projects. In the words of ***Ann***, the IDA director at River University, "*how we deal with different people, develop working relations of open communication, trust, and respect I think gives us the chance to do other tasks and provide support.*" This sentiment was common in all three institutions where participants identified working relations as a method of performing their functions and tasks.

Narrowing further, it could be argued that the flat team structure and open culture of River University and End College enabled their instructional designers to reach out, establish working relations, participate, voice suggestions, and successfully perform supportive functions. Though having similar functions, the way these functions were identified differed between the institutions. Functions were categorized as support and relationship-building roles at River University. The relationship category was identified as a responsive job role at Lane University. Though functions remained the same, the job role differed. But at End College both job categories were merged into a comprehensive support role. Another related difference was the support and relationship-building functions were officially recognized by River University. End College also formally recognized both categories as supportive functions in their job descriptions.

However, the responsive role with functions of informal leadership and being a student and faculty liaison were not recognized or mentioned in official job descriptions at Lane University. This meant that Lane University instructional designers, unlike their counterparts at River University and End College, did not have formal or official authority to engage in these responsive functions. It could mean that unlike universities with team structures which give importance to building relations and helping people, the hierarchical Lane University does not emphasize the importance of building relations. This focus on the support job role strengthens the closed and mechanistic culture at Lane University that focuses on tasks rather than people and relationships.

Unlike their counterparts in River University and End College who saw course design as integral to the development of instruction, instructional designers at Lane University believed that the hierarchical structure and boxed in culture relegated course design, training, and project management functions as minor and unimportant. In the words of **Chloe**, the department's senior instructional designer, course design was *"nothing fancy as design and development."* This meant that course design at Lane University did not involve instructional development and design but routine tasks of writing and proofreading.

Lane University instructional designers relied exclusively on their personal characteristics to circumvent the negative multiple-layered hierarchy to be responsive. This might seem a similarity as even River University and End College instructional designers used personal values to develop working relations, but it was different in approach and focus. Lane University instructional designers rely on individual personal values and beliefs to build relationships not only to manage and complete projects but also to do all their functions and tasks. As described by the learning design director, **Marge**, *"Sometimes just training or writing a course just doesn't cut its just training or writing a cour"* This meant that instructional designers had to go beyond official functions, tap into their personal strengths, and develop an individualized system of navigating to overcome the rigid hierarchy and mechanistic culture. A possible reason for this varied outlook could be that instructional designers, irrespective of working in team structures and cultures or hierarchical structures and cultures, prefer autonomy and maneuvering room to choose how to perform official and unofficial functions and tasks.

Thus, my study concluded that instructional design is a support function. The meaning and scope of support is however diverse and wide. It includes supportive functions of course design, educational technology, training, and project management. This conclusion aligned with several research studies that instructional designers were support staff who helped campus personnel perform their functions (Drysdale, 2018; Fredericksen, 2017; Halupa, 2019; Koszalka et al., 2013). Instructional designers, in accordance with my study findings, were course design and IT support staff with responsibilities of developing and designing effective learning experiences, that is, courses, for face-to-face, online, and hybrid environments (Beirne & Romanoski, 2018; Dick et al., 2005). In fact, scholarly research, as per study findings, discusses the course design support function ranging from research, content writing, proofreading, course formatting, and conducting analysis tasks (Knight & Trowler, 2000; Roberts et al., 1994; Van Rooij, 2010, 2011). In other functions, instructional designers trained and assisted faculty in writing course and learner objectives and deal with LMS updates and navigation. Instructional designers in my study, as well as scholarly studies, were educational technologists with eLearning, multi-media, and LMS tasks. These support tasks and responsibilities for developing, producing interactive videos, audios, checking for web content accessibility, LMS course migrations, and checks (Hansen, 2010; Kang & Ritzhaupt, 2015; Kumar & Ritzhaupt, 2017; Sharif & Cho, 2015).

Discussing the responsive functions of being faculty and student liaison, both study findings and scholarly research identified instructional designers as adaptable, responsive, and supportive personnel who networked, collaborated, and communicated to make sure that students, faculty, and staff have similar expectations. Instructional designers mentored, advised, coached, and built working relations to persuade, influence, and convince campus personnel to adopt course design improvements, strengthen employee engagement through forums of open communication and regular participation (Boling et al., 2017; Gray et al., 2015). In another example, Drysdale (2019) researched the liaison responsive function of informing campus staff about design issues and standards, as well as ensuring that learners and faculty knew and understood each other's needs and expectations.

References

Beirne, E., & Romanoski, M. (2018). *Instructional design in higher education: Defining an evolving field.* Online Learning Consortium. https://onlinelearningconsortium.org/read/instructional-design-in-higher-education-defining-an-evolving-field/

Boling, E., Alangari, H., Hajdu, I. M., Guo, M., Gyabak, K., Khlaif, Z., Kizilboga, R., Tomita, K., Alsaif, M., Lachheb, A., Bae, H., Ergulec, F., Zhu, M., Basdogan, M., Buggs, C., Sari, A., & Techawitthayachinda, R. I. (2017). Core judgments of instructional designers in practice. *Performance Improvement Quarterly, 30*(3), 199–219. https://doi.org/10.1002/piq.21250

Dick, W., Carey, L., & Carey, J. O. (2005). *The systematic design of instruction* (6th ed.). Longman.

Drysdale, J. (2018). *The organizational structures of instructional design teams in higher education: A multiple case study* [Doctoral dissertation, Abilene Christian University]. Digital Commons @ ACU. https://digitalcommons.acu.edu/etd

Drysdale, J. (2019). The collaborative mapping model: Relationship-centered instructional design for higher education. *Online Learning, 23*(3), 56–71. https://doi.org/10.24059/olj.v23i3.2058

Fredericksen, E. E. (2017). A national study of online learning leaders in US higher education. *Online Learning*, *21*(2), n2. https://doi.org/10.24059/olj.v21i2.1164

Gray, C. M., Dagli, C., Demiral-Uzan, M., Ergulec, F., Tan, V., Altuwaijri, A. A., Gyabak, K., Hilligoss, M., Kizilboga, R., & Tomita, K. (2015). Judgment and instructional design: How ID practitioners work in practice. *Performance Improvement Quarterly*, *28*(3), 25–49. https://doi.org/10.1002/piq.21198

Halupa, C. (2019). Differentiation of roles: Instructional designers and faculty in the creation of online courses. *International Journal of Higher Education*, *8*(1), 55–68. https://doi.org/10.5430/ijhe.v8n1p55

Hansen, B. E. (2010). *Characteristics of context for instructional design* [Doctoral dissertation, Capella University]. ProQuest (Publication Number 041).

Kang, Y. J., & Ritzhaupt, A. D. (2015). A job announcement analysis of educational technology professional positions: Knowledge, skills, and abilities. *Journal of Educational Technology Systems*, *43*(3), 231–256. https://doi.org/10.1177/0047239515570572

Knight, P. T., & Trowler, P. R. (2000). Department-level cultures and the improvement of learning and teaching. *Studies in Higher Education*, *25*(1), 69–83. https://doi.org/10.1080/030750700116028

Koszalka, T. A., RussEft, D. F., & Reiser, R. (2013). *Instructional designer competencies: The standards* (4th ed.). IAP.

Kumar, S., & Ritzhaupt, A. (2017). What do instructional designers in higher education really do? *International Journal on E-Learning*, *16*(4), 371–393. https://eric.ed.gov/?id=EJ1155226

Roberts, D. W., Jackson, K., Osborne, J., & Vine, A. S. (1994). Attitudes and perceptions of academic authors to the preparation of distance education materials at the university of Tasmania. *Distance Education*, *15*(1), 70–93. https://doi.org/10.1080/0158791940150106

Sharif, A., & Cho, S. (2015). 21st-century instructional designers: Bridging the perceptual gaps between identity, practice, impact and professional development. *International Journal of Educational Technology in Higher Education*, *12*(3), 72–85. https://doi.org/10.7238/rusc.v12i3.2176

Van Rooij, S. W. (2010). Project management in instructional design: ADDIE is not enough. *British Journal of Educational Technology*, *41*(5), 852–864. https://doi.org/10.1111/j.1467-8535.2009.00982.x

Van Rooij, S. W. (2011). Instructional design and project management: Complementary or divergent? *Educational Technology Research and Development*, *59*(1), 139–158. https://doi.org/10.1007/S11423-010-9176-Z

5 Street-Level Bureaucrats

This chapter explored and discussed the theme of instructional designer job behavior. Instructional designers are considered frontline employees who face dilemmas and go beyond official job functions to improvise and meet diverse client needs. The theme analyzed and evaluated whether the 17 instructional designers, i.e., 5 instructional designers from the Instructional Design and Access (IDA) unit at River University, 7 instructional designers from the Distance Education (DE) department at Lane University, and 5 instructional designers from the Online Learning (OL) department at End College were (a) street-level bureaucrats and (b) coping strategies used by them to deal with tasks beyond their officially assigned functions and duties.

River University

River University instructional designers did not act as street-level bureaucrats. Participants believed the department team structure and culture curbed how they managed finite resources and met diverse client needs. They believed they lacked personal choice and flexible discretion within the tightly circumscribed department structure. Street-level divergence develops when institutional elements of structure, culture, meeting client needs, and finite resources intersect with instructional designer elements of personal characteristics, flexible discretion, and professional development.

Department Structure

This institutional factor referred to how department structure influenced instructional designers' job behavior and performance. It indicated whether department structure made it necessary for instructional designers to go beyond and exercise street-level divergence.

There was consensus among participants that though hierarchical in structure, the IDA unit functioned informally like a flat and flexible team. ***Ann*** explained the IDA hierarchy as a three-tiered structure where the director's position was at the top. The second tier comprises the senior instructional

DOI: 10.4324/9781003426806-5

designer and senior educational technologist followed by the junior educational technologist and Learning Management System (LMS) specialist in the third tier. "*But*" *Ann* emphasized, "*we work as a team. We have a formal hierarchy with specific job roles, but it does not matter.*" She described the team structure as fluid, characterized by two-way open communication, collaboration channels, and a sense of belonging and ownership. The flat team structure enabled them to be involved, share, question, and establish smooth working relations with each other and everyone across campus. "*We know that we can walk over to each other's desk and find out stuff- ask questions,*" *Ann* clarified. She compared the IDA team structure to a beehive. Like bees, instructional designers held different job positions but shared, helped, and worked together for a common goal. To quote *Ann*, "*We have a senior instructional designer, a LMS person, educational technology- they all have different backgrounds and different functions, they have different status in the unit like senior and junior but all work together.*" IDA members shared tasks, functions, and responsibilities and worked towards a common goal of developing instruction.

The formal department hierarchy, according to *Kirk*, existed only for payroll and logistical purposes. *Kirk* believed that the informal IDA team structure was "*a belief not drawn on any document.*" IDA members believed in the team structure. *Ellie* said, "*we share, discuss, ask questions, suggest. We are all equal here.*" The team framework encouraged informality and a relaxed and friendly atmosphere among all IDA personnel.

Culture of Autonomy

Department culture influenced the job behavior and performance of employees. A positive culture indicated an appropriate work atmosphere for employees to go beyond official job descriptions as needed. The flat and flexible IDA team structure ensured a culture of autonomy within the department. Autonomy was defined as the freedom to cut across job roles and share duties. *Ellie* said, "*We all know what's going on and who needs help. How to reach out and help though it may not be our function.*" For example, she spoke about helping her team members with content writing and accessibility issues, even though that was not one of her assigned responsibilities. *Bess* remarked that being aware and helping each other developed feelings of involvement, belonging, and value in every IDA member. She said, "*I think knowing what is going on and why helps us understand and belong to the team, to the university.*"

Expanding on the analogy of bees, *Bess* said that the team structure led to a culture of team learning where "*people were not afraid to make mistakes and own up.*" *Nan*, seconding this view, described such a culture as an open accountable culture where people respected and learnt from each other. IDA members were not afraid to make mistakes and accept their faults.

Nan pointed out that the team learning culture was not about *"who gets it right"* but *"about learning from mistakes and working together"* for designing effective learner-oriented instruction.

Meeting Client Needs

This factor dealt with finding out if instructional designers went beyond their official functions to bend rules, improvise, and adapt policies to meet diverse clients, that is, faculty, staff, and learner needs. Participants saw themselves as supportive personnel who responded to needs and situations and aided campus employees. But they did not think they went beyond official functions to meet client needs.

To IDA personnel, meeting client needs was viewed as understanding, responding, and helping people fulfill their needs and solve problems. **Kirk** however said that meeting client needs was not being responsive and supportive unconditionally all the time. He said, *"being responsive does not mean helping people even when they don't want it or ask for it."* Indeed, university job descriptions spoke about providing *"support when needed."* Being responsive, therefore, meant assessing people's needs and demands and giving help if required. To **Bess**, it meant *"being in the shadow"* and assisting different people through training, consulting, coaching, or solving Blackboard glitches.

Meeting client needs was identified as the primary function and responsibility of IDA personnel. **Nan** said, *"Our work is to help people on campus do their tasks and activities well. And we do this just by doing our functions."* **Nan** paused and continued slowly, *"And sometimes we just have to bend them [functions] so that they get to do their jobs well, you know."* Her comment indicated that the primary role of IDA instructional designers was to help and enable the smooth functioning of other roles, tasks, and activities for their clients. For example, **Nan** and **Ellie** agreed that the formal training function was bent to include tasks of personalized mentoring and coaching to ensure that all learners on campus understood how to navigate Blackboard, upload assignments, and open links. The training was bent to accommodate the needs of all learners and meet their needs and expectations of how to use Blackboard smoothly and successfully. When IDA personnel bent rules, it was to make things easier for clients, not because their needs were ambiguous or unclear.

Other participant responses spoke to the importance and value of having positive working relations with campus people to be able to respond, bend functions when necessary, and meet client needs. **Ann** explained,

> *How we respond is about developing and having that easy relation we can ask questions, clarify issues, discuss. It is giving each other respect and helping them resolve their problems, meet needs.*

Her remark showed that developing and fostering positive and participative working relations was important to providing timely and appropriate help in a suitable manner to clients. ***Ellie***, ***Nan***, and ***Kirk***, all agreed that participative working relations were focused on civility, trust, and respect. ***Nan*** believed a *"working relation with people"* built on trust, free-flowing communication, and respect led to mutual understanding and responsiveness. This easy working relation led to listening, clarifying, discussing to adapt, and adjust functions to meet client needs and issues. These views suggest that meeting client needs is dependent on formal requests for help and official roles of support and relationship, which aligns with participants' prior arguments about the wide range of official roles and corresponding functions that accommodate all methods, tasks, and problem-solving.

Finite Resources

This institutional factor referred to the limited supply of employees, budget, technology, physical workspace, and equipment vs unlimited demand of clients such as learners, faculty, and staff. How instructional designers approached, allocated, and managed limited resource supply to meet unlimited demand influenced their job behavior and performance.

Participants believed that they diverted, shared resources, and went beyond official functions to adjust and adapt limited resource supply to unlimited and continuous demand. Resource allocation and management of limited resources were viewed as a direct consequence of having good working relations with campus personnel. As ***Ann*** and her colleagues noted, having a positive working relationship provided a level of understanding and trust when resources were needed. ***Ann*** explained, *"having a working relation makes it simpler. It's not necessary to argue and justify why and where resources are needed."* Congruently ***Bess*** said, *"The issue of resource management becomes important when we deal with projects."* For example, she spoke about the web content accessibility guidelines (WCAG) project she was involved with. *"My team gets to decide which resource we need like the money, the web technology, and the people- do we need to contact some ed tech guys and for how long?"* Resource allocation and management, she continued became critical when the resource supply was limited but the projects *"just kept on coming."* The resources never kept pace with IDA projects, but they found ways to make it work.

Other participants meanwhile felt that the flat and fluid team structure, culture, and relationship-building functions made it easy and flexible to transfer resources from one project to the other. ***Nan*** attributed the system of resource transfer to the fluid IDA team structure as well as having working relations across campus. She said, *"like I was working on a quality writing standards project, and we ran short of money and the cloud technology.*

So, we just borrowed them from the LMS team." Thus, finite resource management depended on the flexible IDA team structure and positive working relations, which is congruent to the participants' previous assertions about team structure, culture, and relationship-building and support functions leading to autonomy, fluidity, and open communication.

Personal Characteristics

This factor referred to professionalism which comprised individual personal characteristics such as mindset, likes, dislikes, values, and beliefs that influenced job perception, behavior, and performance. Participant responses were divided into two views. The first view revealed no influence of personal characteristics of values and beliefs job attitude, behavior, and performance. **Nan**, **Bess**, and **Kirk** argued that accommodation of personal values such as *"motivation, persistence, empathy, and taking initiative"* were codified in official job descriptions and thus minimized the influence of personal individuality and attitude. **Nan** said, *"All of us are expected to be empathetic, helpful, and flexible in our jobs. It is required, official, you know, and we have to put our personal values, likes behind and just behave and act like the university wants us."* Individual personality quirks such as having a short temper, being quiet, not reaching out, and being helpful did not matter. All IDA staff were expected to display the same personal characteristics. As **Bess** put it, the removal of *"unique behavioral aspects of our personality which sets us apart"* blended all of them into a whole with the same personal characteristics of motivation, empathy, and helpfulness.

The second and opposing view was that personal values shaped IDA team culture and instructional designer function. **Ann** felt that personal beliefs, likes, and dislikes had a major impact on the approach, behavior, and attitude of instructional designers in the IDA team. She said, *"Everything we do depends on us- how we see stuff, our values, and thinking."* Similarly, **Ellie** felt that her personal values and beliefs of persistence, motivation, and empathy propelled her to return to the storyboard and continue discussing her ideas for course development. She observed slowly, *"What makes me say let's do this and design storyboards. What makes me go on repeating myself even though I am shut down many times? Why do I keep on persisting and reaching out like a dog with a bone—gnawing and chipping away continuously?"*

Discrete Flexibility/Flexible Decision-Making

This element was the degree and amount of autonomy and choice exercised by instructional designers to decide, provide support, make adjustments, and improvise on the job. Participant responses indicated a limited maneuvering space to exercise personal autonomy, bend and improvise rules, and make decisions on the job. For example, **Nan** and **Bess** spoke about the centralized flexible team structure and culture where fluid movement, and sharing were accommodated within the system. **Nan** said, *"we share stuff, ask questions, are involved, and it's in the system. And I think this kind of takes away our individuality, the ability to personally decide what to do and when."* **Nan's** remark showed the downside of the flat informal IDA team structure and culture. The team structure and culture covered all aspects of employee flexibility and discretion. **Bess** concurred, *"we don't have the personal space to decide. All the steps are given."* She spoke about working on a Blackboard project where there was no need to choose tasks, resources, or decisions. *"The team knew exactly what to do. Everything was scheduled and stated in the system [There was] no need to think and decide for the team, no need to adjust, plan, and improvise."*

Autonomy in decision-making was further constrained by the university. **Ellie** spoke about how the university *"is closing all holes from where we can wiggle out."* She went on to explain that these *"loopholes and cracks"* were individual personal characteristics that gave instructional designers autonomy, flexibility, and choice to decide and improvise. However, the inclusion of personal characteristics such as anticipation, motivation, and empathy as mandatory job requirements successfully closed those cracks. **Kirk** believed that the flat team structure with channels of open support, participation, and communication left *"little room to use personal choice and judgement"* when faced with issues on the job. Everything was *"covered in the team structure"* leaving IDA members *"little room to improvise and bend rules"* and make decisions.

Professional Development

This factor referred to institutional investment in professional development activities such as refresher workshops which developed a high level of employee engagement and belonging leading to conformity with university systems and functions and minimal job conflict.

IDA participants agreed emphatically that the university invested and provided professional development activities and workshops. For example, the university organized professional development trainings and workshops on the topics of educational technology, quality matters (QM), Blackboard integrations, social and mobile learning workshops, disability awareness, and social learning course design. **Ann**, **Nan**, and **Ellie** saw the university's involvement in providing professional development as a way of ensuring IDA's loyalty and trust. **Ann** felt the workshops, seminars, and trainings not only led to awareness of the latest instructional design knowledge and skill but also as **Ann** put it, *"a way of winning our loyalty and trust."* Professional development signaled a *"caring attitude"* by the university. It assured the university that IDA personnel identified with the caring university.

Professional development was seen as a way of developing employee belonging and teamwork. Speaking of a compliance and web accessibility workshop, **Ellie** said, "*It's like this big forum where we all from different departments and stuff get together, learn and discuss new stuff, we work together as one team.*" Professional development, **Ellie** said laughing, was the university's way of "*telling us we belong here. This is our home.*" Such comments indicated that River University's investment in professional development led to high levels of employee belonging, loyalty, and trust.

Participants such as **Bess** and **Kirk** elaborated further. **Bess** claimed, "*this investment was a smart move.*" The university invested in instructional designer professional growth in the present to reap benefits of it in the future. "*Like if we train and learn new stuff about social learning, we are going to share it on projects and stuff to improve courses.*" She was helped by **Kirk's** argument that investing in IDA staff professional growth meant an assurance that IDA personnel would "*bend over backwards*" for the university. **Kirk** explained, "*I care what happens here as it [River University] cares about my professional growth and development. It is helping me learn and be successful.*" To **Kirk**, it was a mutually satisfying state where both he and the university benefited.

Coping Strategies

Participants believed that they did not have coping strategies as they did not experience conflict on the job. **Bess** and **Kirk** argued that there was no need to go beyond stated official job roles and functions since the university anticipated and provided for solving ill-defined problems with relationship-building functions. **Kirk** said, "*why overthink and do something which is given in the system like mentoring students or leading projects. Everything is covered.*" Functions and tasks of flexible communication, mentoring, coaching, and informal leadership gave instructional designers the opportunity to reach out and work with different people. **Bess** said, "*We help, respond, and meet all campus needs and demands. Just follow our job rules and standards and there is no need to go beyond and do new stuff, you know.*" Similarly, **Ann** stated that establishing and maintaining positive working relations, which she said was a part of their finite resource and project management functions, helped IDA personnel perform supportive and relationship-building functions of project management, educational technology, course design, informal leadership, and faculty and student liaison.

She said, "*if we have that good working relation, we can discuss, share, argue issues, and come up with solutions which are okay for both of us.*" Her comment indicated that smooth and positive working relations were viewed as a forum of open and flexible communication and collaboration. *Ellie* continued with an example of being able to split and share limited resources of personnel and technology on a training project. She said, *"like having a positive working relationship with the professors, IT and admissions staff really helped as I could discuss and make them understand why I needed to borrow these resources."* Shaking her head, she continued, *"sometimes it is hard to work with different people but talking, discussing, reflecting on staff helps, makes everyone get on the same page."*

Thus, it seemed as if all IDA instructional designers had no need for a coping strategy because as *Ann* put it, *"there is nothing to deal with."*

Lane University

Lane University instructional designers seemed to exercise minimal street-level divergence. Participants believed that the negative impact of institutional factors of structure, culture, meeting client needs, and finite resources such as limiting their autonomy propelled them to exercise individual choice and personal characteristics leading to street-level divergence. Instructional design behavior was characterized by poor levels of institutional belonging and trust developed by university non-sponsorship and organization of professional development activities.

Street-level divergence is defined as behavior developed by frontline employees such as instructional designers to meet on-the-job conflicts and dilemmas. It occurs when official institutional job functions do not meet and satisfy client demands forcing instructional designers to improvise and bend official rules to meet client needs, i.e., when institutional narrative factors of structure, culture, meeting client needs, and finite resources intersect with instructional designer narrative factors of personal characteristics, flexible discretion, and professional development.

Institutional and Department Structure

This factor referred to institutional and department structure which influenced employee job performance and behavior. All participants viewed the hierarchical structure of the institution and department as rigid and constraining. *Marge* explained the department's hierarchical structure, *"We have three levels. The director is at the top. Then the senior positions and then fulltime staff of educational technologists, instructional designers, and learning designers."* The third lowest tier of the hierarchy branched into three layers of part-time, regular, and contractual staff of educational technology, learning design, and instructional design. The hierarchy was the supervisory and reporting framework for the department. The director supervised the senior educational technologist and the senior instructional designer. Senior personnel supervised their respective full-time, part-time, regular, and contractual employees. **Chloe** described the department as a *"group of individual units who just do their own jobs."* **Marge** agreed, *"We all stick to our job roles and functions, no interfering and sharing with another."* Such comments indicate a rigid hierarchy with fixed job roles.

Every college, likewise, had its own hierarchical pyramid with faculty inner divisions, administrative employees, and the contracted DE employees on the lowest level. Commenting on the hierarchy within the university, **Adam** said,

> *It's very complex I think like, IT is so layered. Very confusing- Health college again- fulltime tenured faculty, non-tenured faculty, visiting faculty, hospital contractual staff, admin HR guys and then us.*

And every college had its own systems and policies. **Adam** continued, *"It's like having all these mini colleges which are independent"* and have no uniform code for identification in the community. **Beth** agreed that this *"separateness"* was a *"big drawback as people did not realize that the Business school or the IT guys belong to this university."* New students, their parents, and people in the community thought the university's colleges were separate universities by themselves. The lack of a common policy and vision strengthened this feeling.

Department Culture

The institutional factor of department culture referred to department work environments that positively or negatively impacted job performance and behavior. DE participants spoke about the fragmented department culture which created employee friction, resentment, and negativity. The rotational fragmented system as described by **Marge** was contracting two DE employees to a different college every semester. The contracted employees were senior, junior, full-time, contractual, or regular. This system of rotation was also referenced in university job descriptions as DE instructional designers *"being assigned to a college for a fixed time."* **Marge** described the rotational fragmented culture as confusing, *"this constant hopping, no permanence, who to report to- like this ed. tech guy doesn't know whether to report to me, her department senior, college chair, dean- what?"* This *"kind of double reporting"* led to duplication of time and money. Personnel spent time drafting weekly activity logs. *"Time,"* **Marge** said, *"they could spend on real work- course design and stuff."* **Chloe** expressed a similar viewpoint, *"It's like being on the move and just when you get to know how this college works, hey, you are moving again."* **Chloe** complained that constantly moving between colleges at regular intervals did not allow her adequate time to understand the workings and policies of the college. And, after spending time and effort to understand a college policy, she was transferred to another college. To quote **Chloe**, "*it does not give me time to dig my heels in and work.*" These perspectives clearly indicate a convoluted culture characterized by employee confusion, distress, and duplication of time and effort.

Being Boxed In

Boxed in meant being relegated to personal offices with minimal interaction, collaboration, and discussion. It meant working in silos, not being valued, or involved, and being ignored. **Chloe**, **Paul**, **Ted**, and **Adam** believed the boxed in culture had a rippling negative effect. **Chloe** saw the negative effect as "*being shut in our boxes and not encouraged to get out and discuss stuff, give our opinions.*" To **Paul** and **Ted**, the boxed in culture was a system of one-way communication and collaboration. **Paul** explained that "*everything flowed in one way from top to bottom, all communication, instructions, and directives, we just shut up and follow orders.*" He went on to admit that he had tried once to discuss a quality writing issue and had been rudely cut off.

> *I emailed her [professor] and she was like-just do what I say and no need to discuss- I emailed her again and soon I was called in by HR and given a warning* [laughing and shaking his head] *and now I simply do what is told, I get the message, loud and clear- no discussion that's it.*

Paul's experience indicated the culture of being boxed in had been imbibed as official cultural policy where even the HR department issued warnings if anyone attempted to, as **Paul** put it, "*get out of our boxes and discuss or collaborate.*" There was a definite lack of autonomy of movement and expression which as **Ted** emphasized, "*makes us sort of invisible. Like what we say, think, our knowledge is useless.*" The boxed in culture had a wide-reaching negative impact on instructional designer thought and perception about their knowledge and skills.

One-Way Communication

Another feature of the fragmented department culture was a one-way communication channel where there was no exchange or discussion of ideas. **Paul** argued one-way communication discouraged discussion, "*a respectful give and take*" of ideas. There was no open two-way communication, which created frustration among DE personnel. **Paul** explained, "*It's like we have all these cool ideas and can help but we are shut off.*" **Sally** reiterated this view that the one-way communication led to a lack of involvement, "*we don't know what is happening, not allowed to ask questions and so feel kind of* *cut-off."* This was contrary to the description of the DE instructional designer in Lane University's official job descriptions as *"a multi-tasking instructional designer, effective communicator, collaborator, highly participating in all campus operations."* In fact, **Adam**, **Beth**, and **Chloe** argued that the system of one-way communication of receiving instructions had created a narrow and disinterested instructional designer. **Beth** colorfully described it as *"see everything, hear everything but never say anything and just close your eyes, ears, and mouth."* Her remark indicated a communication system of receiving information and directives and not exchanging information or ideas. Mutual discussion, sharing, questioning, clarification, and collaboration were not allowed. To **Adam,** the one-way system created *"narrow instructional designers with blinders"* whose outlook and vision had been reduced to remaining in their boxes and mindlessly performing instructions and assigned tasks. These views suggest a top-down one-way communication channel where instructional designers are at the lower end receiving and following instructions, which is comparable to participants' previous descriptions about having no say in deciding training topics, project issues, and following directives flowing from top executive leaders.

Meeting Client Needs

This institutional factor referred to whether frontline employees went beyond official job functions and bent rules to meet clients' diverse needs. Participants claimed that they went beyond stated official job descriptions and performed responsive functions to solve and fulfill diverse client needs. **Marge** described meeting client needs as being responsive, adaptive, and open to change. Responsiveness was anticipating what was needed and *"doing everything possible"* to meet clients' changing needs and demands. **Marge** argued that meeting client needs in a rigid closed culture with strictly demarcated job roles and functions was not easy. She said, *"Everything is so tight here and it is not easy to go beyond what we are supposed to do and help faculty resolve writing or D2L linking issues, stuff which is not covered in our official functions."* **Paul** agreed that all DE personnel, irrespective of their job roles and functions, performed responsive tasks such as *"We meet with faculty and learners every day and know their little problems. Why is this D2L interface not working properly? Make it work properly. Help me make my D2L course compliant."* Such comments showed that responsiveness was dependent on instructional designers' willingness and initiative to step outside their boxes and interact with clients.

To other participants such as **Adam**, **Beth**, and **Chloe**, responsiveness was being adaptive and open to changing situations, work environments, and institutional protocols. **Adam** observed, *"We have to bend policies and cut corners, you know, make the surrounding suitable to solving the problem and that's okay.*

It's all about resolving everyone's issue in whatever possible way." **Beth** described DE personnel as being adaptive support staff who "*whatever college they are in at that time*" provided timely, long-term, effective solutions that were adaptive not only to client needs but also to institutional norms, culture, and policies. Her remark indicated that responsiveness did not only mean responding to client needs and providing solutions. It was providing solutions that were adaptive and long-term. **Adam** saw them as "*chameleons*" who changed and adapted their functions to respond and blend seamlessly with changing work environments and client needs. Apparently, meeting client needs is dependent on instructional designers' personal values and mindset which enables them to bend and adapt existing rules, develop a conducive environment, and go beyond official protocols and resolve client issues.

Finite Resources

The institutional factor of finite resources was about employee flexibility and autonomy to allot and manage a limited resource supply to meet unlimited demand. DE participants, contrary to their previous assertions about lack of autonomy, claimed that they had the autonomy to divert, borrow, and share resources to meet changing client needs. **Chloe**, **Marge**, and **Paul** believed their unofficial responsive functions combined with their personal attitudes helped them exercise flexibility and autonomy in allocating and managing resources. **Marge** explained, "*I think how we respond is on us. What we think, our beliefs, cutting corners, being flexible, adjusting to make sure everyone has resources.*" **Paul** explained his experience of diverting money officially allotted for a D2L integration project to fix online grading issues. He believed he had been able to do that only because he had developed "*a kind of interaction and working relation with them [project members]*." And he warned that establishing and developing working relations in a closed hierarchical structure was challenging. "*We really need to have a working relation to make sure people understand why we are using stuff not put for this task.*" His remark highlighted the element of positive working relations as a vital component of finite resource management.

Smooth finite resource management was dependent on the development of positive working relations with different campus personnel. **Beth** believed that having "*good working relations*" with different campus personnel helped her reach out, persuade, and share limited resources. She said, "*sometimes the projects drain too much of resources and we don't have enough for other tasks like doing D2L training on our own time.*" Examples she shared of being creative with limited resources were borrowing cloud workspace including digital memory and diverting money to develop interactive Open Educational Resource (OER) technology and links of Six Sigma leadership training for an organizational behavior course. **Sally** described "*the matter of having working* *relations*" as a "*huge challenge.*" She said that the rigid one-way communication channel of "*shutting up and doing instructions*" made it difficult to "*to discuss and persuade people to share resources.*" Developing and maintaining a working relation, **Sally** noted "*is a personal thing. I mean how we keep up that relation is on us, how we deal with people, what we say and think.*" Finite resource sharing and management were realized because instructional designers relied on their personal characteristics.

Personal Characteristics

Personal characteristics were described as instructional designer professionalism which influenced job attitudes, choice, behavior, and performance. DE participant responses revealed that they exercised individuality and choice to go beyond official roles and provide immediate help, despite negative messaging they received regarding being silent, following instructions, and doing as they were told. **Marge**, **Ted**, and **Sally** spoke about the robust influence of individual personal characteristics on the identity, job behavior, and performance of instructional designers at Lane University. **Marge** said,

> *What we do daily on the job, the way we deal with everyone on campus, even how we see instructional design I think is because of our beliefs. Like what makes us respond to different learner and faculty needs? Why don't we just do our jobs and shut up?*

She believed that personal values, likes, and dislikes "*guides our behavior and responsiveness on the job.*" For example, why do DE learning designers help faculty with writing and compliance issues before solving a D2L problem? Clearly, personal likes and dislikes were directing instructional designers' behavior of choosing to resolve faculty writing issues before D2L technical issues.

Personal characteristics were viewed as requisite behavioral traits for performing responsive roles as street-level bureaucrats. **Sally** and **Ted** spoke of resilience and empathy values which propelled them to perform functions not required by the university. **Sally** lauded her attitude of "*keep on going*" and "*understanding, bending over backwards*" in making her empathize with learners and staff. Such personal values enabled participants to initiate channels of open discussion and participation among staff.

Individual personal characteristics were seen as having more weightage and importance and allowed them to work around the one-way communication, fragmented hierarchy, and a boxed in culture. **Adam**, **Beth**, and **Sally** believed that individual personality elements of persistence, respect, desire to help, and motivation influenced DE personnel to develop working relations with campus personnel. **Adam** said, "*It is how we feel, what is important to us,* *how we maintain working relations with different faculty. How we continue to make noises and kind of communicate."* ***Adam's*** comment hinted that DE instructional designers relied on their personal behavioral traits to get around the rigid hierarchical system of one-way communication and being boxed in to establish working relations and have some type of open communication. Though not ideal, it enabled DE instructional designers to have some degree of autonomy and choice. ***Beth*** agreed that it was their personal attributes, *"what we think, how we think which makes us find ways to reach out and talk stuff and build good working relations."*

Autonomy/Flexible Decision-Making

This instructional designer factor refers to the level of autonomy and flexibility exercised by frontline employees to decide, improvise, and go beyond official functions. Participant responses indicated they had autonomy and flexibility in decision-making, which appears contradictory to their previous assertions about limited autonomy, constrained functions, and the expectation that they should simply follow orders. It could be that participants had developed ways to exercise autonomy, influence, and flexibility despite the negative culture. ***Marge***, ***Chloe***, ***Adam***, and ***Ted*** spoke about the influence of their personal mindset and values which influenced how and why they made and implemented decisions. ***Ted*** said, *"I feel it is our thinking and approach that gives us the ability to make decisions, how to help."* The use of the word *ability* suggested an overwhelming influence of personal characteristics that shaped instructional designer decision-making and consequent job behavior and performance. Likewise, ***Chloe*** felt that personal values and beliefs of willingness to help, persistence, and empathy enabled them to reach out, try to communicate, build working relations, discuss, and influence decision-making. To ***Adam*** and ***Chloe***, decision-making was having the autonomy to share, question, and exchange ideas and suggestions to make the right decision. Such views bring out the strong influence of personal characteristics on discrete flexibility and decision-making which aligns with participants' previous arguments about the heavy influence of personal traits on job behavior and performance.

Professional Development

This instructional designer factor spoke to how university non-sponsorship and organization of professional development activities led to low levels of employee trust and belonging and led to street-level divergence. Lane University instructional designers said they did not feel a part of the university. This low and negative feeling of belonging and trust was because Lane University did not organize, sponsor, or invest in professional development activities for

DE staff. Official job descriptions place the onus of professional development participation on the individual employee. Per one of the job descriptions, the DE staff is expected to

> *continually develop professional skills through personal initiative. Learning design and skills trainings, presenting at conferences, meetings, and events, writing case studies, academic paper; to become certified in QM.*

From this job description, one can infer that participation in professional development activities such as going to conferences or workshops was dependent on individual desire and choice.

Participant responses were divided into two views. The first view held by **Ted**, **Adam**, **Marge**, and **Paul** was that Lane University's non-sponsorship of professional development activities led to poor levels of belonging. The second view held by **Chloe** and **Sally** was that professional development participation was a personal choice and responsibility and should be independent of university sponsorship.

Sponsorship and organization of professional development activities such as workshops and seminars were regarded as an unnecessary expenditure by the university. **Ted** said that Lane University did not believe in investing money and time in professionally developing its instructional designers. **Adam** explained with the example of the QM workshop. He felt that it would have been beneficial for the university if all DE personnel had gotten QM certified at the same time. In **Adam's** words, *"Just one big workshop for a week and we all get it but now getting it on our time is difficult."* **Ted**, who had taken a week of personal leave to attend QM workshops, saw the non-sponsorship of professional development by the university as *"unprofessional, and inconsiderate."* He felt that the university was shirking its responsibility of *"taking care of employee professional growth and development."* He went on to explain, *"I don't feel like giving my 100% anymore. They [Lane University] doesn't care about me, my career goals."*

University non-sponsorship of professional development activities led to feelings of detachment, disinterest, and lack of belonging among DE staff. **Marge** and **Paul** reiterated **Ted's** argument that the university did not care about their professional development. To quote **Paul**, *"I don't feel like I belong here, I mean they don't care how I develop professionally, learn new stuff, nobody bothers and that's not right. We work here and so shouldn't the university care about us?"* These views suggest a mutually beneficial situation where employees experience belonging and trust only when the university cares about their professional growth and development by sponsoring and organizing such activities.

In contrast, the other two participants believed participation in professional development was an individual personal choice. **Chloe** regarded professional development as a personal career development and improvement initiative that was independent of university sponsorship. She said, "*I am on LinkedIn and other professional sites and that's how I meet people, network, and write papers with them.*" She believed that her initiative and motivation had helped her attend and participate in professional development workshops on her own time. **Sally** concurred that the university was not responsible for ensuring employee professional growth. She said, "*We work here and that's it. Why should the university do everything? Some things, I feel should be left to us. We should have a say in how we want to professionally develop like our goals, certifications.*" **Sally's** remark indicated that perhaps instructional designers welcomed Lane University's non-sponsorship as a way of exercising individual discretion and choice. These views indicate that though Lane University instructional designers expect the university to care about them by investing in professional development activities, the absence of university involvement in such activities is seen as an opportunity to realize and exercise personal choices and autonomy. It suggests that these instructional designers are rationalizing university non-involvement in professional development. They are making excuses for the university's behavior and justifying it as an opportunity for personal initiative.

End College

Analysis of participant responses indicated they did not act as street-level bureaucrats. Street-level divergence is framed by institutional framing elements of institutional structure and culture, meeting diverse client needs, finite resources, and instructional designer factors of personal characteristics, flexible discretion, and professional development. All participants vouched for a positive and flat team structure and culture with features of functional fluidity and positive communication. Interestingly, participants also commented about how the tightly circumscribed team structure and culture also limited the sharing of finite resources, going beyond and meeting client needs, and flexible decision-making. Participant responses recorded a heavy and positive reliance on individual personal characteristics. This reliance on personal traits was viewed as being influential in the development of working relations and finite resource management. Participant responses indicated low and negative levels of belonging and trust due to campus non-involvement and organization of professional development activities.

A Team Structure and Culture

This institutional element refers to the institutional and department structure and culture that impact the on-the-job behavior and performance of instructional designers. Participant responses indicated the institutional and department team structure and culture impacted the way they approached and performed their functions. **Tina** detailed the structure of the college as being divided into teams at both the campus and department levels. **Tina** said, "*it's a team everywhere, I mean every college and admin unit, whether it is HR, Health department or us.*" The OL team was two-tiered with the director and assistant director sharing the "*top positions.*" The second tier comprised all OL team members who despite regular, part-time, contractual, full-time status, or having different functions were viewed as having equal status.

The OL department's flat and flexible team structure was characterized by a fluid, open, and positive culture. **Jay** and **Sid** spoke about the lack of hierarchical lines of reporting and supervision which advocated equality and informality. **Jay** said, "*We work together. All of us, part-time, full-time, regular, temporary- we are equal whether it is the director, or anyone else, or me. We tell each other what we're doing, what we are working on.*" **Sid** concurred that he "*did not have a boss.*" He described his superior to be on an equal status as him. "*I can just walk up to him and ask questions, discuss, and argue,*" he said. "*It's all friendly and informal here.*" **Tina** and **Liz** commented on the department's cross-functional two-way communication and collaboration which enabled free and participative exchange of information, ideas, and suggestions. "*The structure I think creates a kind of fluid system where we flow across roles and functions, talk, reflect, and are involved in everything that goes on.*" **Liz**, on her part, spoke about the feeling of value created by the open communication channel. She shared, "*we feel valued as professionals. All of us are on the same footing and that gives a sense of importance.*"

Functional Fluidity

Another feature of the flexible team framework was functional fluidity or interdependence. Functional fluidity, according to **Tina**, was based on the equal status of every OL team member which gave them the freedom to "*move about and poke their noses*" in all functions. This was evident in **Liz's** remark that despite her official role as a learning designer, she was involved in all functions. "*I do a bit of everything, LMS, ed tech, and mentoring. Our roles are not fixed,*" she said. **Sid** believed the fluidity "*gets us out of our boxes from time-to-time and participate.*" His remark indicated that the functional fluidity experienced by OL members was not continuous. Instead, they often kept to themselves, performed their functions, and participated in team functions and activities occasionally. **Sid** went on to explain,

> We have our specific roles and functions and we usually do them, stick to our desks but if needed, when asked we have the freedom to go about and help in other functions. No formality but it's not like we don't have our structured functions, we do.

Sid's explanation suggested that though organized as a flexible team structure, every OL member mostly kept to their specific functions and only emerged out of their "*box*" or office to help others in their work when asked by other team members. There was an interplay between the OL staff's specific tasks and functions and their teamwork.

The reason for the functional fluidity of the OL team was the interconnectedness of the functions. Referring to her experience, **Liz** said, "*We have our tasks and responsibilities for the day, but it is hard to just do one task as everything is so connected.*" Intertwining her fingers, she continued that every instructional design task was connected to the other and needed the other task to be performed simultaneously or in sequence for the successful completion of the function. For example, writing, course formatting, and uploading the course on LMS were three separate tasks but had to be done together to design a course.

Team Culture

The OL team was characterized by a culture of positive communication, empowerment, and trust. **Tina** credited the department culture to the flat team structure where all personnel, irrespective of their official job titles, were considered equals. She said, "*How we are in the department I think like we know we can talk free, ask questions and discuss because we work as one-as a team.*" To **Carla**, the open team culture meant a lack of stiff formal communication. The channel of communication was open and positive without fear of negative consequences, "*what is gonna happen if I disagree, give my opinion.*" Positive communication, **Tina** said was a two-way, free, and participative channel of interaction which was "*talking, writing, body, and face expressions. It is letting the other person know what you are thinking, feeling.*" To these two participants, positive communication depended on the flat and open team structure and culture characterized by autonomy and free discussion without fear of negative consequences.

To some other participants, positive communication meant equality, respect, and trust. **Liz** said, "*positive communication is when the person talking is on the same level as the other person, is equal.*" Positive communication worked only in a flat team structure where all members enjoyed equal status. **Sid** and **Carla** believed that positive communication was about mutual respect, appreciation for each other's knowledge and skill, and empowerment. **Sid** said, "*it is based on knowledge, skill, expertise and so I think it gives confidence and is so empowering.*" He went on to explain that having the relevant academic knowledge and skill not only "*makes people listen to you*" but also builds working relations with campus personnel and initiates change. **Carla** noted, "*communication where you know your stuff develops people's trust and respect.*" These views suggest that positive communication is an umbrella that includes trust, respect, and empowerment and leads to change in thinking and action.

Meeting Client Needs

This institutional factor referred to going beyond official functions and tasks to meet clients' diverse needs. It meant bending rules and established official norms and improvising to resolve issues and problems. OL participants believed they did not go beyond official functions and tasks, bend rules, or improvise to meet clients' diverse needs and issues. But they also believed they did reach out, respond, and help campus personnel resolve issues and meet needs.

Meeting client needs was a part of the OL staff's official job descriptions which included becoming aware of client issues, responding, and providing timely support to resolve them. **Tina** felt the support functions of being student and faculty liaison, informal leadership, course design, and training met and satisfied campus personnel needs and resolved issues. She said laughing, "*See we don't need to go beyond and satisfy clients. It's all there in our functions.*" **Carla** went on to explain her own experience of collaborating to design a management course. "*I worked with a management instructor and had to do everything to meet his need of a quality compliant course on Moodle (LMS).*" To do all tasks of analysis, writing, formatting, compliance, and accessibility checking **Carla** believed she had to perform her designated official functions and not go beyond the official job framework. **Sid**, **Liz**, and **Jay** agreed that college job descriptions covered all instructional designer functions to meet diverse client needs. **Jay** said, "*everything is given in clear terms—how and when to mentor, streamline, integrate tech, write new courses. We don't have to think and improvise or do anything, it's all there.*" These End College OL staff members believed they had no reason to improvise, or bend or break, the rules on behalf of clients because everything they needed to do was already built into their job descriptions and official functions.

Finite Resources

The institutional factor of finite resources explored how frontline employees balance and manage finite resources to meet a continuous unlimited demand, respond, and solve all issues. For OL participants dealing with finite limited resources meant following official job functions. **Liz** explained, "*We don't have to bother. It's all there in the system. What to do, how to share, streamline.*" She laughed and continued that the college had made "*everything simple and straight.*" **Jay** concurred, "*We just have to do our jobs, and everything is laid out. The way to communicate, work with each other, share resources, integrate same ed tech for many things and stuff.*" Such views suggested that finite resource allocation and management was a linear and simple process of following official job roles and functions.

Other responses highlighted positive working relations with campus personnel as the foundation for finite resource management. **Sid** said, "*I think having working relations with everyone on campus is important, to known what they want and what we can do about it.*" He believed that working relations ensured that OL personnel met all campus needs and resolved all issues without hassle. Likewise, **Carla** felt that since resources on campus were limited, everyone had to "*keep in touch with each other to discuss, ask*" to select, share, borrow, and transfer resources to resolve all campus issues. For example, having limited digital cloud space to meet the online needs of all courses. As **Carla** noted,

> *Every course needs digital memory and space, you know for links to other sites, eLearning segments, and integrations. But only a limited amount is there and so we have to make do with that. And so, we get together, discuss, explain, have that trust and respect stuff going. We really have to step up and get that relationship going. Then I think it is easier to say, hey we need to share this ed tech.*

Comments of these two participants indicated that OL personnel were responsible for taking the initiative and developing positive working relations to manage limited and finite campus resources. Thus, OL instructional designers share, borrow, distribute, and manage finite resources by simply performing official tasks and functions which includes developing a positive and two-way communication and participative working relations.

Personal Characteristics

This instructional designer factor revolves around the degree to which individual personal characteristics of values, beliefs, likes, and dislikes influence and shape instructional designer job behavior and performance. OL participants believed strongly that their personal characteristics influenced the way they approached their work, behaved on the job, and performed their functions. **Liz**, **Tina**, and **Jay** felt that personal values, a mindset of resilience, and a go-getter attitude shaped the way in which they viewed their tasks of LMS, writing, training, and mentoring. **Liz** said, "*How we see things, what is important for us and why I think that matters a lot, like why I feel helping people and getting things done on time is important.*" **Tina** spoke about how taking the initiative on projects, reaching out, and building working relations with different people depended on her personal mindset and attitude. "*You might be shut down. It really is about my inner drive which keeps me going,*" she noted, while **Liz** shared about how individual likes and dislikes influenced which tasks and projects were done first. She shared, *"I like creating storyboard and writing instruction more than LMS tasks of uploading courses. So, I do writing and storyboard tasks first and before schedule [laughing] I always do LMS last."* But **Liz** went on to explain, someone else might prefer doing LMS tasks before content writing and storyboarding.

Personal values of motivation, persistence, and being helpful were viewed as shaping interaction, collaboration, and building working relations. **Sid** felt that his inner desire to help people and his persistence influenced him in his methods of interaction and collaboration. *"How I reach out, keep at it, discuss and work with different people to have a good working relation is all on me."* Nodding his head in agreement, **Jay** felt that personal beliefs of empathy, kindness, and patience helped OL personnel develop positive working relations and perform functions of mentoring, training, and course design. While **Carla** along with **Sid** felt that though personal values were integral to every person's behavior, instructional designers tended to use them more. **Carla** attributed the reason for instructional designer's reliance on personal characteristics to their direct proximity to clients. She noted, *"We interact directly with professors, students, instructors, other staff, and it could be why we get more ways to resolve problems, work with everyone, and do stuff not in our functions, you know?"* All these views revealed the frontline employee status of instructional designers who worked directly with campus personnel and relied heavily on individual personality characteristics.

Flexible Discretion

Known as flexible discretion-making, this institutional factor referred to on-the-job autonomy which enabled frontline employees to bend rules and share, collaborate, and influence decision-making. Participant views were divided on the issue of flexible discretion and decision-making. **Jay**, **Tina**, and **Sid** believed the positive and flat team structure limited their ability and capacity to move and share functions and responsibilities. In fact, **Jay** stated that the OL team structure was *"rigid and tight with everyone sticking to their assignments and tasks."* He went on to explain that their ability to move, or as he put it *"flow into each other's business was kind of frowned upon."* Team roles and functions were fixed and tightly bound. Jay continued that OL members could only *"step outside their boundaries when called or requested and this is rare."* Likewise, **Sid** said, *"We just don't go about sticking our nose into everything. We do our functions and when asked we do go beyond and help."* Thus, flexible discretion appears to be dependent on requests for help which contradicts participants' previous assertions about the interconnectedness of team roles which provides for fluid movement across team roles and functions without the need for help requests.

The other participants believed that apart from requests for help which allowed OL staff to exercise autonomy, flexible decision-making was dependent on individual personal characteristics. **Carla** believed the OL team relied on their personal values, mindset, and beliefs to "*help and be there for each other and campus I think.*" Exercising their personal traits enabled them to make "*quick decisions on the spot*" and not go "*through team hierarchy and stuff.*" Talking about her experience of deciding which Moodle integration to use, **Carla** said, "*I had to be patient, persistent, and go back to it even after being told not to bother. I think my personal thing of not giving up ultimately won. I got to decide and do it.*" **Liz** also emphasized personal values of "*being civil to each other, being tolerant I think helps in working things out and making decisions.*" Such views indicated how instructional designers' personal values and beliefs framed flexible decision-making. Thus, it appears that flexible discretion and decision-making are framed and influenced by requests for help and individual personal characteristics.

Professional Development

This factor referred to the level and degree of belonging and trust felt by frontline employees because of campus-sponsored and organized professional development activities. High levels of employee belonging indicated conformity with institutional systems and a subsequent lack of conflict leading to a lack of street-level divergence and vice versa. OL participants claimed to have low levels of employee belonging and trust because of non-involvement and sponsorship of professional development activities.

End College considered professional development an individual and personal initiative. **Tina** observed that participation in all educational technology, course design, and Moodle (LMS) workshops, seminars, and webinars was left to the discretion and choice of the OL instructional designer. To quote **Tina**, "*Whether it is getting certified in Quality Matters [QM], cloud and web technology, new Moodle updates.*" She continued that the college did not get involved in any aspect of "*sponsoring or even organizing these workshops and it's a big blow.*" **Tina** believed that this "*kind of detached and uncaring attitude like you do your own thing and then come back to use it in your work is so not cool.*" Echoing her sentiments **Liz** felt the uncaring attitude sent out a message to the OL department that the college was not interested in their professional growth and development. The college was interested in the results, or as **Liz** colorfully put it, "*fruits of our labor but not the actual process of getting to the fruit.*" She shared an example of attending a couple of workshops and seminars on WCAG updates. Pursing her lips, **Liz** went on that taking the initiative to attend these workshops on her own time "*put a dent in how I feel about this place.*" **Liz** did not feel a part of the college as it did not care about how she expanded and improved her knowledge and skills.

Explaining further the consequences of not being cared for, *Jay* said, "*It's like if the college doesn't care about us, why should we care about the college?*" He argued that if the college wanted them to have feelings of loyalty, ownership, and belonging; the college needed to invest in their professional development. He shared his experience of taking leave from work to attend a workshop on 3D cloud technology organized in another state. Screwing his eyes, *Jay* said, "*why should I use the 3D stuff for their courses? They didn't help me, so why should I? They don't care, so why should I care?*" *Jay's* argument revealed a clear division of thought with End College as *them* standing opposite OL instructional designers who identified as *us*. Participants' remarks clearly indicated the disinterest and uncaring attitude of End College had contributed to feelings of resentment and anger among OL personnel.

Coping Strategies

This element explores the coping strategies and methods street-level bureaucrats use to deal with on-the-job dilemmas and conflicts. Participants expressed confusion about engaging in coping methods to deal with on-the-job dilemmas. In fact, *Tina* questioned, "*Dealing with what?*" She went on to state that she did not have any coping methods as she did not experience any on-the-job conflict. In her words, "*I don't think we have dilemmas because everything is so clear, I mean our functions, our duties. What we do every day. We just need to stick to our functions, and everything works out just fine.*" *Tina* believed that strict adherence to official functions and duties was adequate to successfully meet all campus issues and create any on-the-job conflict. This sentiment appears contradictory to participants' previous comments about building positive working relations and relying heavily on personal characteristics to deal with the management of finite resources, making decisions, and having the autonomy to move across team functions without requests for help.

The presence of a clear coping strategy was evident in other responses. *Sid* felt that following official functions and tasks of "*communicating, mentoring, training, developing good working relations*" was a "*kind of coping strategy.*" These functions and tasks were, in fact, tools and methods that "*sort of guided what we have to do, why and how to resolve all issues.*" *Liz* elaborated with an example of the official training function which comprised multiple tasks such as mentoring, communication, advising, collaboration, and active listening. These tasks made OL personnel aware of problems, opened channels of information and idea exchange, and "*got them to work together, discuss, and come up with solutions.*" Such views indicated that End College provided coping strategies within its official system. OL instructional designers coped with daily responsibilities and client needs by following official functions and tasks.

Street-Level Bureaucrats 93

Analysis and Conclusion

Findings and analysis across the three institutions revealed a strong similarity in the existence of street-level divergence. Instructional designers, whether it was in the team structure at River University and End College, or the rigid hierarchical Lane University, exercised minimal to no level of street-level divergence. Instructional designers, whether in team-oriented River University and End College, or the rigid hierarchical Lane University, seemed to exercise minimal to no street-level divergence. And this is puzzling as conducive team structures and cultures with two-way positive communication, autonomy, or functional fluidity, as per academic research lead to street-level divergence (Ashbaugh, 2011; Drysdale, 2018; Miller & Stein, 2016). But findings align with scholarly literature that instructional designers in hierarchical structures and closed cultures do not lead to street-level divergence (Ashbaugh & Piña, 2014; Knight & Trowler, 2000).

This could be because instructional designers in all institutions rely heavily on their job descriptions to guide their job behavior, approach, work, and function. They strictly follow official job functions, and this is evidenced in my study. There is a complete alignment between official job descriptions and instructional designers at River University and End College, while Lane University uses these official job descriptions to justify performing additional tasks and functions such as responsive functions. Official job descriptions are the foundation of how instructional designers behave on the job.

What instructional designers do on the job and how they interact depends on the institutional and department culture. For example, instructional designers at River University and End College develop positive working relationships which gives them the autonomy to practice positive finite resource management. As seen in the study findings, the team hierarchy is influencing these instructional designers to maneuver and develop positive working relations to share, transfer, and borrow finite resources. Similarly at Lane University, the hierarchical closed culture is forcing these instructional designers to develop working relations, rely on personal values to circumvent the hierarchy, and make campus personnel aware of their presence and functions.

Similarly, instructional designers in all three institutions believed they responded and met client needs, managed finite resources, and exercised judgment and choice in making decisions. The manner and method of response were also similar, that is, relying on personal characteristics to establish working relations to share, discuss, manage finite resources, and exercise flexible discretion and choice in making decisions. This is puzzling as to why instructional designers belonging to team structures with open cultures that provided conducive work environments for street-level divergence relied on building positive working relations to manage finite resources, practice autonomy, respond, meet client needs, and exercise judgment to make decisions. A possible reason could be that detailed job descriptions of River University and

End College, which described all functions and tasks minutely curbed their autonomy and choice to respond, make decisions, share, discuss, and manage finite resources. Though not explicit, it was evident that the flat team structure and culture in both these centralized institutions created a tight team hierarchy which in the words of **Ellie, the educational technologist at River University**, "*left little room to wiggle.*" Consequently, instructional designers in both these institutions were confined to strict adherence to official functions and left with little need and room to go beyond and improvise to help and meet client needs. This strict adherence to job roles and functions was identified as a coping strategy, which, as expressed aptly by **Sid, the learning designer at End College**, "*sort of guided what we have to do, why and how to resolve all issues.*" Though rigidly following job roles and functions limited instructional designers, it was also a coping strategy that gave them the official job tools and methods to respond and meet client needs.

At Lane University, personal characteristics such as willingness to help, motivation, persistence, resilience, and empathy led instructional designers to view negative systems positively and develop working relations to share, transfer, manage resources, exercise choices, and judgments to influence people in decision-making. Personal beliefs, as **Adam, the instructional designer and technology specialist** put it, enabled them to "*continue to make noises*" and make people aware of their presence and suggestions.

This similarity of reliance on personal characteristics and working relations seems to indicate that instructional designers in all three institutions balance their institution's structure and culture with their individual personal characteristics to exercise street-level divergence. At River University and End College, instructional designers relied on personal values to build positive working relations and exercise street-level divergence when they found the team structure and culture tight and narrow. At Lane University, instructional designers were using their personal values such as willingness to help, persistence, and inner drive to circumvent the rigid hierarchy and culture to exercise street-level divergence. As such, these instructional designers had a common coping strategy of building working relations to deal with on-the-job dilemmas. A possible reason for the robust influence of personal characteristics over that of institutional structure and culture could be that instructional designers, whether in teams or rigid hierarchies like to move and maneuver space to exercise autonomy, choice, manage resources, practice judgment, and make decisions. Over time, they had figured out that relying on their personal values was perhaps the best way to go about gaining legitimacy and being more visible. It could also be that being support staff with limited power and authority, they had to draw upon their values of motivation, persistence, and resilience to develop working relationships to get anything done.

Another similarity was the instructional designer factor of professional development. Instructional designers at the rigid hierarchical Lane University, and the flexible team-oriented End College believed that professional development was a personal responsibility and choice. These instructional designers felt that improving their knowledge and skills was a matter of personal discretion which was independent of institutional authority. They further argued that their low level of belonging and trust was fueled by institutional non-involvement in their professional development.

A major difference was the development of institutional and instructional designer factors of management of finite resources, flexible discretion, and decision-making in the flat and team-oriented institutions of River University and End College. River University instructional designers believed the flat tightly circumscribed team structure created a team hierarchy that limited sharing, borrowing, transfer, and management of finite resources as well as flexible decision-making. However, End College instructional designers stated the team hierarchy limited their desire for functional fluidity, autonomy, and sharing. The rigid team hierarchy confined them to their specific team functions wherein they could only participate and help when asked. Functional fluidity was conditional, and this restricted flexible discretion and decision-making.

Another striking difference was the instructional designer factor of professional development at River University, Lane University, and End College. River University was invested in the professional development of its instructional designers and subsequently developed high levels of employee belonging and trust. This led to high levels of employee satisfaction and street-level divergence among River University instructional designers. However, instructional designers at End College experienced low levels of employee belonging and trust leading to low street-level divergence. This was because despite having a team structure and culture which believes in employee professional development, End College did not invest in it. However, expectedly the hierarchical closed Lane University did not invest in professional development either, leading to low employee belonging and trust. Though instructional designers relied on their personal values to participate in professional development activities, their focus and perception were different. While End College instructional designers demanded college involvement in professional development and used their personal values as a contingency option; Lane University instructional designers saw this non-involvement as an opportunity to exercise choice and autonomy in selecting how to improve their knowledge and skills. As aptly explained by **Sally, the educational technologist at Lane University**, "*Why should the university do everything? Some things, I feel should be left to us. We should have a say in how we want to professionally develop like our goals, certifications.*" Again, the reason could be that instructional designers irrespective of institutional structure and culture prefer to choose, decide, and respond.

The study, therefore, concluded that instructional designers are not street-level bureaucrats. To summarize, instructional designers exercised minimal to negligible street-level divergence. For the most part, as seen in my study, instructional designers in all three institutions rigidly adhered to their functions.

Instructional designers at River University and End College felt their job descriptions to be holistic and comprehensive detailing every function, task, and responsibility. These instructional designers believed that they met diverse client needs, solved problems, and practiced good management of finite resources by following university-outlined functions and tasks. They did not feel the need to go beyond and bend rules and improvise to meet client needs.

While at Lane University, instructional designers admitted to doing unofficial functions to respond to and help people. But their responses implied that though they were performing these additional functions not listed in their job descriptions, they did not seem to be experiencing any dilemma. They were simply doing these additional unofficial functions to help campus personnel. It was a way of dealing with the rigid hierarchy and closed culture such as developing working relations in a culture of shutting up and following instructions. This suggests that perhaps institutional culture more than daily on-the-job conflict frames and shapes how instructional designers approach their work and behave on the job. This conclusion contradicts and questions the street-level bureaucracy theory which holds that frontline employees experience on-the-job conflict and so act as street-level bureaucrats (Cooper et al., 2015; Frisch Aviram et al., 2021).

Instructional designers seem to be frontline employees and have direct contact with campus staff and learners, but their frontline status is questionable. For instance, as per study findings, instructional designers spoke about being indirect organizational contributors who remained in the background and helped other campus personnel to visibly contribute. Another explanation could be that perhaps instructional designers in universities react and/or interact with their clients differently as compared to instructional designers in other industries. Instructional designers working in universities do not interface with the public, as per the foundational assumption of street-level bureaucracy theory (Maynard-Moody et al., 2003; Moore, 1987). They interact with faculty, learners, and other campus staff. They provide support to design courses and remain behind the scenes. This could be affecting the manner of their interaction and consequent job behavior. Maybe there is something different about frontline workers in public universities that the street-level bureaucracy theory doesn't apply to them.

References

Ashbaugh, M. L. (2011). *Online pedagogical quality questioned: Probing instructional designers' perceptions of leadership competencies critical to practice* [Doctoral dissertation, Capella University]. ProQuest. https://www.learntechlib.org/p/118534/

Ashbaugh, M. L., & Piña, A. A. (2014). Improving instructional design processes through leadership-thinking and modeling. In B. Hokanson & A. Gibbons (Eds.), *Design in educational technology* (pp. 223–247). Springer. https://doi.org/10.1007/978-3-319-00927-8_13

Cooper, M. J., Sornalingam, S., & O'Donnell, C. (2015). Street-level bureaucracy: An underused theoretical model for general practice? *British Journal of General Practice, 65*(636), 376–377. https://doi.org/10.3399/bjgp15X685921

Drysdale, J. (2018). *The organizational structures of instructional design teams in higher education: A multiple case study* [Doctoral dissertation, Abilene Christian University]. Digital Commons @ ACU. https://digitalcommons.acu.edu/etd

Frisch Aviram, N., Beeri, I., & Cohen, N. (2021). From the bottom-up: Probing the gap between street-level Bureaucrats' intentions of engaging in policy entrepreneurship and their behavior. *The American Review of Public Administration, 51*(8), 636–649. https://doi.org/10.1177/02750740211023597

Knight, P. T., & Trowler, P. R. (2000). Department-level cultures and the improvement of learning and teaching. *Studies in Higher Education, 25*(1), 69–83. https://doi.org/10.1080/030750700116028

Maynard-Moody, S. W., Musheno, M., & Musheno, M. C. (2003). *Cops, teachers, counselors: Stories from the front lines of public service*. University of Michigan Press.

Miller, S., & Stein, G. (2016). Finding our voice: Instructional designers in higher education. *Educause, 10*. https://er.educause.edu/articles/2016/2/finding-our-voice-instructional-designers-in-higher-education

Moore, S. T. (1987). The theory of street-level bureaucracy: A positive critique. *Administration & Society, 19*(1), 74–94. https://doi.org/10.1177/009539978701900104

6 Organizational Contribution

According to SLB theory, frontline employees contribute to organization development which is one of the job goals that determines development of street-level divergence. This element explores whether and how street-level bureaucrats contribute to organizational growth and development. Street-level bureaucrats contribute highly and positively to organizational development and vice versa.

River University

All five participants in the IDA department instructional designers believed they contributed to organizational development. Participants described their organizational contribution in terms of their job role and function. To **Ann** and **Nan** their organizational contribution meant performing course design activities. **Ann** described her organizational contribution as *"designing effective learner-oriented courses."* She believed that IDA's contribution to organization development and growth was measured and assessed by the number and quality of designed face-to-face, online, and hybrid courses. Functions of content writing, research, content organization, compliance, and accessibility checks assured the university of smooth and efficient instruction. This, said **Ann**, *"helps our university promote its learning programs and courses [and] enroll new and diverse learners."*

Educational technologists **Kirk** and **Ellie** defined their organizational contribution as promotion and development of educational technology and LMS. **Kirk** said that his contribution to organizational growth and development meant *"functions of educational technology, LMS checks and integrations."* **Ellie** clarified that it meant researching, adapting, and aligning the university to new and dynamic educational technology changes. She said, *"it is knowing what apps, software are out there and looking at ourselves and seeing what is missing and then filling that technology gap."* She gave the example of Blackboard updates and integrations like games, eLearning apps, and links. *"Such alignment I think benefits us,"* she explained. *"It makes our courses more advanced. This is more attractive to learners who want everything tech online."*

DOI: 10.4324/9781003426806-6

Successfully responding and meeting client needs was another facet to how some participants viewed organizational contribution. To quote *Ellie*, "*how we contribute I feel depends on how well we resolve issues, reach out to people, [how we] meet student, faculty needs.*" Instructional designer organizational contributions depended on performance of responsive and relationship-building functions included in official job descriptions. *Bess* claimed that her "*daily tasks of solving LMS glitches, mentoring, plug all loopholes and we can progress and develop faster.*" Her comment indicated that her daily functions of solving LMS issues and mentoring clients ensured that all client issues were met and solved. This, she believed, helped in keeping university systems, online courses, and Blackboard running smoothly. Seconded by other participants she continued, "*just by doing our assigned functions I think we contribute and take the university forward.*" They contributed to the organization's advancement by simply doing their jobs. Such views indicated that IDA instructional designers believed they contributed towards organizational development by following and performing official functions and assigned tasks.

Lane University

The seven participants in the DE department, as per their job descriptions and interviews, agreed that they actively contributed to the resource technology and learning of the university. Indeed, job description references of expectations for "*active collaboration and support for contribution to resource technology and learning*" provided ample empirical support for this belief. All participants felt they contributed to the development of Lane University, even when the university did not value their contributions. For example, contrary to participants' negative critique, the fragmented rotational system was viewed as a major positive influence on degree of organizational contribution. *Marge* believed the rotational fragmented structure and culture created avenues for DE instructional designers to "*contribute to every college during different times.*" The lack of permanence or, as she put it, "*constant hopping*" between different colleges was an advantage as it helped DE instructional designers know "*what was missing to develop uniformity in policies and systems.*" Expanding on this advantage, *Paul* believed this constant fluidity gave them "*a golden chance to see what that college is doing different*" that distinguished Lane University from other universities in the state. The system did not create fragments but bought different colleges together with "*same policies, norms, and technology*" under "*one banner of [Lane] University.*"

Organizational contribution was influenced by instructional designer's personal characteristics. To *Beth*, her personal beliefs of empathy, respect, and tolerance towards others helped her view the negative boxed in culture which limited autonomy, participation, and choice as an opportunity to contribute to "*overall learning and course design.*" **Sally** felt her personal values of "*persistence, resilience, desire to help*" enabled her to establish a positive image, identity, and bring about changes in LMS and eLearning systems despite the lack of permanency and consequent inability to establish a foothold in any college due to the rotational culture. The views of these two participants indicate that instructional designers use their personal values to change a negative system and method into a positive opportunity to meaningfully contribute.

To **Ted** and **Adam**, organizational contribution was balancing official university systems and functions with unofficial university functions and guidelines. **Ted** described it as "*playing in the middle,*" that is, doing and following university established systems of rigid hierarchy, rotational fragmented and boxed in culture and at the same time going beyond official protocols and performing individual responsive functions to meet diverse client needs and contribute to university development. Overall, instructional designer organizational contribution appears to be a mix of official functions and unofficial functions whose performance is influenced by personal characteristics.

End College

All five participant responses were confusing and clear at the same. **Carla** and **Liz** were confused as to why they should contribute in any manner to the development, growth, and expansion of the college. **Carla** argued, "*But why should we worry about it? They have leaders for it, college board, vision, strategic goals, and plan.*" She said that the OL department was "*not in any leadership position*" to make policy decisions and change college's vision or mission. Talking about her role, **Carla** said she was not involved in college policy or planning. She was only responsible for course design and implementation of existing and new courses. **Liz** agreed, "*We should not do something that we are not supposed to do.*" These views indicate that organizational contribution was considered the sole forte and responsibility of college leadership which appears contradictory to the official instructional designer role of informal leadership.

Other participants believed that they helped faculty and staff contribute indirectly to college recruitment, course and educational technology development, and teaching. **Jay** said, "*We don't help directly. I mean we are behind the scenes and help others do their work right. I guess that's our contribution.*" **Jay's** remark indicated that OL personnel did contribute, but indirectly by performing official support functions such as course design, training, and educational technology. **Tina** elaborated further, "*We are a service support department. Our job is to support and help others, like designing good courses for faculty. We don't contribute I think but yeah, we definitely help others contribute.*" She spoke about contributing to increasing admission and retention rates of adult learners by helping instructors develop interactive learner-oriented graphic design certification courses for adult learners. While **Sid** remarked about contributing on projects, *"especially web compliance training projects. I mean my knowledge about the web guidelines, how I train, ask questions helps faculty and staff do stuff better."* Such comments identified how OL personnel viewed themselves as indirect organizational contributors.

Analysis and Conclusion

An in-depth analysis found that findings across the three institutions revealed that most instructional designers saw themselves as organizational contributors. For River University instructional designers, which had a team structure and culture, and for Lane University instructional designers which had a rigid hierarchy, organizational contribution meant performing official functions, tasks, and duties and directly contributing to their institution's growth and development. For example, **Ann** and **Nan**, instructional designers at River University, saw their organizational contribution as simply doing their assigned function of designing effective courses. According to **Ted**, the learning designer, Lane University, organizational contribution was achieved by simply following all organizational functions, systems, and protocols.

But End College instructional designers saw their contribution as indirect. These instructional designers believed the performance of their functions and tasks helped other campus personnel contribute to organizational growth and development. In the words of **Jay**, the Instructional design and technology coordinator at End College, *"We don't help directly. I mean we are behind the scenes and help others do their work right. I guess that's our contribution."* Strangely, some instructional designers felt that they did not contribute at all to college policy, development, or planning. Organizational contribution, according to them, was the sole responsibility of the college executive leadership board. **Liz**, the department learning designer, put it as *"We should not do something that we are not supposed to do."*

Another similarity was that instructional designers in all three institutions used their personal characteristics such as willingness to help, resilience, and empathy to develop working relations and establish participative communication and collaboration channels to go beyond official rules and functions, develop street-level divergence, and contribute to their institutions. For example, instructional designers at River University and End College relied on personal values and beliefs of persistence and motivation to develop positive working relations which enabled them to understand, respond, and help people solve their issues. Congruently, personal characteristics influenced how instructional designers in Lane University navigated and viewed the negative hierarchy and closed culture in a positive light to contribute to organizational development. An apt example was provided by **Marge**, the DE department's instruction design director, who felt that the negative rotational fragmented culture and consequent lack of permanence was an opportunity to know *"what was missing to develop uniformity in policies and systems."*

A possible reason for this influence of personal characteristics could be that instructional designers tend to define organizational contribution narrowly. They seem to think that organizational contributions should be big, visible, and impactful. Just performing their job functions and responsibilities was not enough. Personal values, beliefs, and attitudes gave that *extra boost* to make their contributions big and important. For example, instructional designers at all three institutions used their personal characteristics such as persistence, empathy, and inner drive to help campus personnel resolve their issues and problems. Personal values were the tool which enabled them to navigate team or rigid hierarchies, develop autonomy, and establish open communication that highlighted different personnel issues.

Undoubtedly, as per my study, instructional designers, as established in scholarly research, contributed to organization development (Ashbaugh, 2011; Drysdale, 2018; Koszalka et al., 2013). The scope and range of instructional design contribution differed from direct to indirect, and sometimes questioning reason for contribution since it was not an official function. Direct organizational contribution, as per study findings and academic research, referred to performing course design and development functions (Ashbaugh, 2011). In her study, Ashbaugh found that instructional designers performed critical and important roles in designing and developing learner-oriented courses. To do so, they performed tasks of content writing, research, embedding educational technology, and LMS training. While at End College, some instructional designers believed that they should not contribute as it was not their job function. This suggests that these instructional designers depend heavily on their job descriptions to determine their functions, what they should do and not do.

Indirect organizational contribution, meanwhile, referred to helping campus faculty perform their functions and contribute to organizational growth and development (Fredericksen, 2017; Halupa, 2019). Instructional designers performed various supportive and responsive functions which enabled campus personnel such as faculty, admissions, and human resources personnel to interact, teach, and recruit students successfully. These supportive functions, as outlined in many studies, comprised helping faculty develop blueprints, write performance and learner objectives, select educational technology and social learning apps (Gray et al., 2015).

References

Ashbaugh, M. L. (2011). *Online pedagogical quality questioned: Probing instructional designers' perceptions of leadership competencies critical to practice* [Doctoral Dissertation, Capella University]. ProQuest. https://www.learntechlib.org/p/118534/.

Drysdale, J. (2018). *The organizational structures of instructional design teams in higher education: A multiple case study* [Doctoral Dissertation, Abilene Christian University]. Digital Commons @ ACU. https://digitalcommons.acu.edu/etd

Fredericksen, E. E. (2017). A national study of online learning leaders in US higher education. *Online Learning, 21*(2), n2. https://doi.org/10.24059/olj.v21i2.1164

Gray, C. M., Dagli, C., Demiral-Uzan, M., Ergulec, F., Tan, V., Altuwaijri, A. A., Gyabak, K., Hilligoss, M., Kizilboga, R., & Tomita, K. (2015). Judgment and instructional design: How ID practitioners work in practice. *Performance Improvement Quarterly, 28*(3), 25–49. https://doi.org/10.1002/piq.21198

Halupa, C. (2019). Differentiation of roles: Instructional designers and faculty in the creation of online courses. *International Journal of Higher Education, 8*(1), 55–68. https://doi.org/10.5430/ijhe.v8n1p55

Koszalka, T. A., RussEft, D. F., & Reiser, R. (2013). *Instructional designer competencies: The standards* (4th ed.). IAP.

7 Conclusion and Implications

To briefly recapitulate, this qualitative study investigated three higher educational institutions in the US to find out instructional designers' perceptions: (a) about instructional design, roles, and daily functions, (b) coping mechanisms, i.e., street-level divergence of instructional designers, and (c) how instructional designers contribute to organizational development, through the theoretical lens of street-level bureaucracy (SLB). I conducted semi-structured virtual as well as in-person interviews, depending on participant convenience and choice, with 17 instructional designers: 5 from River University, a four-year degree-granting university located in Midwest US, 7 instructional designers belonged to Lane University, a four-year degree-granting university in southwest US, and 5 instructional designers were from End College, a two-year technical college in southwest US. Below is a tabulated summary (Table 7.1) of the study's findings.

The BIG Conclusion

The study's findings, analysis, individual conclusions reflected a contradictory and confusing scene of instructional design behavior, and function. Instructional designers, as evidenced in my study, felt that they improvised and went beyond official job functions. Yet, they firmly believed that they were not street-level bureaucrats. So, what were the factors responsible for influencing instructional designer on-the-job behavior and action of bending departmental norms and roles and yet function smoothly within the official job framework designed by the higher education institution?

Instructional Designer Job Behavior Is Influenced by Institutional Culture

Instructional designer job behavior is influenced and framed by institutional culture (Paais & Pattiruhu, 2020). For instance, instructional designers at Lane University strictly adhered to their culture of being boxed in which led to minimal participation, collaboration, and communication. The culture of working

DOI: 10.4324/9781003426806-7

Table 7.1 Summary of Findings

Theme	River University	Lane University	End College
Instructional Design	Mismatch ADDIE vs Not ADDIE	Alignment Design Process—emphasis on ed. technology-learner influence	Alignment Design process Theory + design—instructional design
Job Roles and Functions	Alignment Support Role—4 functions Relationship-building Role—2 functions	Partial Alignment Official Support Role—3 functions Unofficial Responsive Role not in job descriptions—3 functions	Alignment Comprehensive Support Role—supportive + relationship building/responsive functions
Street-Level Divergence	None	Minimal	None
Institutional Factors			
Structure and Culture	Team structure Culture of autonomy—flexibility, two-way communication	Rigid hierarchy Rotational and fragmented culture Boxed in—minimal participation One-way communication	Team structure Functional fluidity Positive communication
Meeting Client Needs	No need	Going beyond-unofficial responsive functions	No need
Finite Resources	Positive working relations Good working relations	Working relations Unofficial responsive functions Working relations	No need Positive working relations
Instructional Designer Factors			
Personal Characteristics	Inclusion in official job descriptions Removal of individual personal behaviors	Strong influence Working relations	Strong influence Direct client contact
Flexible Discretion	Flexible team structure Personal characteristics	Personal characteristics Working relations	Conditional Personal characteristics
Professional Development	University involvement High employee engagement Mutual benefit	No university involvement Low employee engagement Dependent on personal initiative	No university involvement Poor employee engagement Dependent on personal initiative Them vs Us
Coping Strategy	Follow official functions	Unofficial Responsive functions	No conflict Official functions
Organizational Contribution	Job role and function	Personal characteristics Official + unofficial	Why contribute? Indirect

in silos, as per academic literature, led to job behaviors of not involved, and being detached (Lowell & Ashby, 2018). But surprisingly, this closed culture was pushing instructional designers to develop working relations and establish a communication channel. The closed culture of shutting up, simply following instructions, and nodding in agreement to everything was fostering job behaviors of autonomy, choice, personal initiative, and participation.

The findings contradict Hupe and Hill (2007) research assertion that instructional designers working in decentralized closed cultures experience negligible participation and interaction. Lane University instructional designers engaged in responsive functions because their institutional culture restricted them to narrow supportive roles of course design, educational technology, and training. The culture led them to reach out, respond, and meet diverse client needs. Congruently, the top-down one-way communication channel, which as per academic literature curbed discussion, sharing, autonomy, choice, exchange of ideas and information, led to autonomy, participation, and collaboration (Gray et al., 2015; Knight & Trowler, 2000).

However, as evidenced in my study and refuting academic literature, open cultures, which ostensibly led to instructional designer autonomy, participation, and two-way positive communication, in fact curbed autonomy, personal initiative, and choice of instructional designers at River University and End College (Destler, 2017; Drysdale, 2018; Intentional Futures, 2016; Trekles, 2011).

Instructional Designer Job Behavior Is Influenced by Personal Characteristics

Instructional designer personal characteristics influence and shape their job behavior. Personal values, beliefs, mindsets, likes, dislikes, and approach influence how instructional designers interact, communicate, make choices, respond, and meet diverse client needs. This aligns with scholarly research that instructional designer level of interaction, communication, collaboration, and autonomy depended on their individual mindset, personal values of empathy, resilience, and desire to reach out and help (Ashbaugh, 2011; 2013; Gardner et al., 2018).

At River University and End College, personal attributes of taking initiative, being persistent and resilient despite criticism and rejection, enabled instructional designers to maneuver. Park and Luo (2017) spoke about how personal characteristics of motivation and diligence enabled instructional designers in centralized systems to choose, prioritize, and manage finite resources. Similarly in the hierarchical Lane University, as per academic research, personal characteristics of persistence, resilience, motivation, and helpfulness influenced how instructional designers responded, cut corners, improvised, and went beyond official job functions (Ashbaugh & Piña, 2014;

Boling et al., 2017; Campbell et al., 2009; Gray et al., 2015). In fact, personal values of moral purpose and truthfulness guided the autonomous, pro-choice attitude where instructional designers navigated and managed to overcome a closed one-way communication channel to share, discuss, and manage finite resources and make decisions. These instructional designers despite working in a culture of being a cog and performing tasks mindlessly managed to establish and maintain working relations to communicate, collaborate, and provide unconditional support to campus people (Hupe & Hill, 2007).

Implications

The study's findings, analysis, and conclusions provide an interesting insight into instructional designer on-the-job behavior and performance. They help to unpack questions: what do study results mean for instructional design practice?

Implications for Practice and Policy

This qualitative study researched two centralized and one decentralized university, all located in different parts of the US. The sample size of 17 instructional designers with corresponding job descriptions provided a robust foundation to explore practice and policy implications for instructional design in higher education.

Developing a Formal University Definition of Instructional Design

Academic literature as well as study findings indicates that instructional design lacks a singular holistic definition (Gustafson & Branch, 2002; Merrill et al., 1996; Munzenmaier, 2014; Reiser & Dempsey, 2012). Perhaps university administrators could establish an instructional design board to provide a singular formal definition of instructional design for their university. This would remove ambiguity and minimize any chance of a misalignment between university-assigned functions and typical instructional design functions. Having an instructional design board would also streamline university job descriptions and clarify roles, tasks, and responsibilities.

Developing Awareness about Instructional Design

University administrators should organize workshops and other discussive forums which inform and educate campus personnel about the meaning, scope, role, and importance of instructional design. Doing so, perhaps, will help campus personnel, that is, faculty, staff, and learners understand, acknowledge, and appreciate the role and expertise of the instructional designer and what they can contribute. Organizing these information workshops could benefit the university by ensuring that all campus personnel understand and realize that minor tasks, such as editing, proofreading, and uploading courses to the learning management system (LMS), help in designing effective courses which align with learner expectations (Ashbaugh, 2011; Bawa & Watson, 2017; Richardson et al., 2019). The workshops could ensure staff recognize and understand instructional designers as integral and valuable employees who can provide critical support in all course design and teaching functions.

Dismantling or Changing Dysfunctional Cultures

Instructional job behavior and consequent job performance are dependent on the institutional culture. Thus, university administrators should be aware of faulty dysfunctional cultures and aim to change or dismantle them. Doing so would positively impact instructional designer work, attitude, and behavior. Perhaps university administrators should consider appointing independent consultants to examine the culture of the institution and how it affects the job behavior and performance of instructional designers. For example, dismantling the rotational and fragmented institutional culture at the decentralized Lane University which has a negative impact on behavior and attitude of instructional designers.

A Conscious Move to Develop Hybrid System

University administrators should consciously blend the positive elements of team systems with the positive elements of hierarchical systems. Positive flat team structures with open cultures which afford autonomy, two-way communication, and teamwork (Drysdale, 2018; Magruder et al., 2019). Team systems with their detailed job descriptions that list every role and function could blend with hierarchical systems which provide wide maneuvering room for instructional designers to exercise their unique personal characteristics and forge their own path of coping. University administrators could merge the detailed job description element of team structures which minimize ambiguity. These job descriptions are highly descriptive and provide for every task and responsibility. In fact, adherence to these job descriptions makes it simple and easy for instructional designers to help campus personnel, respond, and contribute to overall course design and development (Ashbaugh, 2011; Hansen, 2010). As remarked by one of the participants at River University, *"why overthink and do something which is given in the system."* Thus, higher education administrators could merge these elements together and establish a system, wherein instructional designers follow detailed job descriptions, and yet have maneuvering space to exercise and maintain their unique individuality. They should dig deeper and deliberately develop hybrid systems which encourage and foster instructional designer individual unique personal characteristics.

Investing in Professional Development Continually

University administrators should invest and organize professional development activities such as workshops, refresher classes, and seminars for instructional designers on campus regularly as an integral part of staff development. Such initiatives, as per theory, boost instructional designer level of involvement, engagement, belonging, and increase positive behavior and attitude toward the institution (Davidovitz & Cohen, 2022; Destler, 2017). Study findings show that River University instructional designers who enjoyed university involvement in professional development activities experienced high employee engagement, belonging, and trust. These instructional designers believed the university cared about their professional growth and well-being and were willing to work hard. They considered the university their "*home*" and cared for its development. Comparatively, Lane University and End College instructional designers experienced poor employee engagement and belonging due to university non-involvement in professional development. To minimize such negative behaviors and attitudes, perhaps university administrators should organize and initiate professional development for instructional designers. Doing so might develop positive behaviors of belonging, involvement, and caring about university.

Theoretical Implications

My study examined the implications of using the SLB theory to explore and understand instructional designer job behavior and performance. The study's conclusions and findings suggest that the SLB theory is not apt to explore and explain how instructional designers behave on the job. The theory is not relevant as instructional designers in all three universities did not consider themselves to be street-level bureaucrats.

Critiquing the Street-Level Bureaucracy Theory

This study exposed the internal contradictions and inconsistencies of the SLB theory. The theory assumes that all frontline employees are street-level bureaucrats (Frisch Aviram et al., 2021; Magnusson, 1981; Moore, 1987). This assumption, however, is challenged by my study findings and conclusions which show that instructional designers, at River University, Lane University, and End College, despite being frontline employees, are not street-level bureaucrats. They do not experience any conflict on the job and conform to institutionally defined functions, culture, and norms. In fact, these instructional designers rely heavily on their institutionally defined roles and functions to do their work, develop cultural norms, and sometimes do some extra tasks. At River University as well as End College, instructional designers seemed to welcome this alignment between official job functions and their actual on-the-job functions. To them, everything was provided for in the system and they did not have to overthink and exert themselves. Similarly, Lane University instructional designers followed their official supportive job functions and used the job functions to justify their additional functions of mentoring and responding to campus personnel needs. In all three cases, the frontline job behavior of instructional designers refutes the SLB theory.

The theory assumes that the presence of a finite resource supply to meet diverse unlimited client needs leads to employee conflict and resentment (Evans, 2010). The theory, thus, does not consider that usually public organizations have scarce resources which are not properly allocated between organizational personnel and could lead to employee resentment, competition, and angst (Tjosvold & Poon, 1998). But, as evidenced by my findings, though instructional designers at all three institutions experienced finite resource supply and unlimited client demand, they do not seem to face any conflict and resentment. In fact, it led them to develop ways to distribute the limited resources between various client needs and projects and practice smooth finite resource and project management. Finite resources developed working relations, communication, and collaboration.

The theory assumes that frontline employees who exercise street-level divergence contribute to the organization. But, as seen in my study all instructional designers, whether they exercised street-level divergence or not, contributed to the organization. River University and End College instructional designers were not street-level bureaucrats but contributed to organizational development.

Apparently, instructional designer job behavior cannot be explained through the theoretical lens of SLB. Perhaps academicians should consider alternative theories which might explain why frontline employees such as instructional designers do not experience job conflict and exercise minimal to no street-level divergence.

Examining Instructional Designer Job Behavior and Performance through the Lens of Organizational Culture Theory

The heavy influence of culture as a key driving factor in shaping how instructional designers approach their job role, function, behave on the job, and perform should perhaps be viewed through an alternative theoretical lens of organizational culture. The theory of organization culture advocates that behavior, motivation, and work performance are driven by a "*pattern of shared basic assumptions*" and behaviors learnt by a group of people through "*external adaptation and internal integration*" of environment, culture, and personal values to solve problems (Paais & Pattiruhu, 2020; Schein, 2010, p. 18). Instructional designers at all three institutions seem to have common philosophies leading to similar behaviors and thoughts. For example, at River University and End College, the culture of openness led to common shared behaviors and assumptions of equality, flexibility, and positive working relations. While at Lane University the closed culture led to common behaviors and practices of engaging in unofficial responsive functions and developing working relations. Institutional culture thus seems to influence and shape how this group of professionals, i.e., instructional designers, react, approach institutional systems, and behave on the job. These instructional designers, as per theory, espouse common beliefs and values of relying on personal characteristics, responding, and helping to solve client diverse needs (McDermott & O'dell, 2001).

This suggests that perhaps the theory of SLB used as the theoretical lens to view and understand the job behavior and performance of instructional designers is narrow with a myopic vision. A broader theory with a holistic outlook needs to be considered which views instructional job behavior and performance in a cultural context. This could provide understanding into the why, what, and how of instructional designer on-the-job behavior and performance. For example, the fragmented and rotational culture at Lane University seemingly leads to a lack of permanence but surprisingly is viewed as a positive opportunity to develop uniformity on campus. These instructional designers have internalized the negative cultural philosophy and developed common behavioral patterns of engaging in working relations, relying on personal characteristics, and viewing the institutional negative system in a positive light.

Similarly at River University and End College, instructional designers relied on common personal values to develop positive working relations to practice good finite resource management. These instructional designers adapted their behavior with external institutional culture and at the same time internalized the cultural philosophy of team flexibility and autonomy to develop common patterns and norms of positive working relationships, and finite resource management.

Implications for Future Research

A major implication of this research for future studies would be to find out if gender influences instructional designer job behavior. Out of the 17 participants interviewed in this study 11 were female. Gender did form part of my interview protocol as an icebreaker question but was not investigated as a factor impacting instructional designer on-the-job behavior and performance. It would be interesting to study its effect on instructional design definition, job roles and functions, and on-the-job behavior. An expansion of this study could be to find out if there is a difference in the perceptions of female vs male instructional designers. The study could also be broadened to explore the impact of race and ethnicity. Along with gender, this study did collect participant data about race and ethnicity, but only to ease into the interview. These factors were never explored and could prove to be an interesting extension of this study. It would benefit scholarly literature to understand how and why race and ethnicity of instructional designers impact their perceptions about instructional design, job roles and functions, job behavior, and organizational contribution.

This study explored instructional designer street-level divergence at three public higher education institutions. It would be interesting to empirically study instructional designer street-level divergence at private universities. It would benefit instructional design scholarly literature to compare how instructional designers in both public and private universities behave on the job.

Another possibility could be researching this same issue in an international context, that is, exploring how instructional designers in foreign universities view instructional design, job roles, functions, and job behavior. Another future study could be to concentrate on corporate, military, and industry sectors which employ full-time instructional designers. It would be interesting to study how instructional designers working in these sectors view instructional design, job roles, and functions. Another possible study could be to examine the issue of funding of instructional design practice. Does funding impact perception of instructional design?

Wrapping Up

To summarize, this book adapted a qualitative doctoral research study to a book format, and I believe, it provides an illuminating interesting snapshot of how instructional designers work, behave, and interact with each other, faculty, staff, and students in higher education. My empirical investigation of 17 instructional designers at varying levels at three public higher educational institutions in different parts of the country showed emphatically that instructional designers do not view themselves as street-level bureaucrats. Though they were frontline workers who interacted with clients (faculty, staff, students) daily they believed that tasks performed by them did not fall outside the purview of their official university-assigned job roles and functions. As such these instructional designers did not practice street-level divergence, but tasks outside their official job function and responsibility were merely a part of their comprehensive job role. As seen in the individual findings, analysis, and individual findings as well as group conclusions, instructional designer work and behavior was guided and framed not by client demand, resource availability, or client satisfaction but organizational culture and norms.

Indeed, it can be successfully concluded per my theoretical implications, instructional designer function and behavior should be considered from the perspective and theoretical lens of organizational culture. Per interview excerpts, instructional designers at the three universities considered their work and behavior as following organizational culture, mission, and vision. This perspective was further strengthened by the overwhelming influence of instructional designer personal characteristics. However, what was not apparent was whether individual personal characteristics influenced behavior and approach toward organizational culture and function, or was it organizational culture that enabled an instructional designer's personal characteristics to become dominant? Thus, the study refuted the theoretical lens of SLB as a way of understanding instructional design function and behavior.

The study ended with practical and policy implications—what higher educational institutions can and should do to utilize the wide and diverse repertoire of instructional knowledge and skills to benefit organizational growth and productivity. Individual findings and corresponding conclusion cemented the argument that instructional designers viewed themselves as organizational contributors, but perhaps this contribution could be increased and diversified if these implications are followed as suggestive guidelines. Future implications provided suggestions for future research studies and opportunities. But this qualitative study was, in the words of Denzin & Lincoln, (2011) *"not absolute."* Research can never be an end itself but only give rise to more research paths and avenues. Similarly, my qualitative study was a small and essential investigative effort in a long and confusing quest to understand the concept, function, and work of instructional design including those of its practitioners.

References

Ashbaugh, M. L. (2011). *Online pedagogical quality questioned: Probing instructional designers' perceptions of leadership competencies critical to practice* [Doctoral dissertation, Capella University]. ProQuest. https://www.learntechlib.org/p/118534/

Ashbaugh, M. L. (2013). Personal leadership in practice: A critical approach to instructional design innovation work. *TechTrends, 57*, 57–82. https://doi.org/10.1007/s11528-013-0694-5

Ashbaugh, M. L., & Piña, A. A. (2014). Improving instructional design processes through leadership-thinking and modeling. In B. Hokanson & A. Gibbons (Eds.), *Design in educational technology* (pp. 223–247). Springer. https://doi.org/10.1007/978-3-319-00927-8_13

Bawa, P., & Watson, S. (2017). The chameleon characteristics: A phenomenological study of instructional designer, faculty, and administrator perceptions of collaborative instructional design environments. *The Qualitative Report, 22*(9), 2334. 10.46743/2160-3715/2017.2915

Boling, E., Alangari, H., Hajdu, I. M., Guo, M., Gyabak, K., Khlaif, Z., Kizilboga, R., Tomita, K., Alsaif, M., Lachheb, A., Bae, H., Ergulec, F., Zhu, M., Basdogan, M., Buggs, C., Sari, A., & Techawitthayachinda, R. I. (2017). Core judgments of instructional designers in practice. *Performance Improvement Quarterly, 30*(3), 199–219. https://doi.org/10.1002/piq.21250

Campbell, K., Schwier, R. A., & Kenny, R. F. (2009). The critical, relational practice of instructional design in higher education: An emerging model of change agency. *Educational Technology Research and Development, 57*(5), 645–663. https://doi.org/10.1007/s11423-007-9061-6

Davidovitz, M., & Cohen, N. (2022). Playing defence: The impact of trust on the coping mechanisms of street-level bureaucrats. *Public Management Review, 24*(2), 279–300. https://doi.org/10.1080/14719037.2020.1817532

Denzin, N., & Lincoln, Y. (2011). Introduction: The discipline and practice of qualitative research. In N. Denzin & Y. Lincoln (Eds.), *The SAGE handbook of qualitative research* (pp. 1–20). SAGE.

Destler, K. N. (2017). A matter of trust: Street level bureaucrats, organizational climate and performance management reform. *Journal of Public Administration Research and Theory, 27*(3), 517–534. https://doi.org/10.1093/jopart/muw055

Drysdale, J. (2018). *The organizational structures of instructional design teams in higher education: A multiple case study* [Doctoral dissertation, Abilene Christian University]. Digital Commons @ ACU. https://digitalcommons.acu.edu/etd

Evans, T. (2010). Professionals, managers and discretion: Critiquing street-level bureaucracy. *The British Journal of Social Work, 41*(2), 368–386. https://doi.org/10.1093/bjsw/bcq074

Frisch Aviram, N., Beeri, I., & Cohen, N. (2021). From the bottom-up: Probing the gap between street-level bureaucrats' intentions of engaging in policy entrepreneurship and their behavior. *The American Review of Public Administration, 51*(8), 636–649. https://doi.org/10.1177/02750740211023597

Gardner, J., Chongwony, L., & Washington, T. (2018). Investigating instructional design management and leadership competencies–A Delphi study. *Online Journal of Distance Learning Administration, 21*(1), 1–21. https://eric.ed.gov/?id=EJ1173467

Gray, C. M., Dagli, C., Demiral-Uzan, M., Ergulec, F., Tan, V., Altuwaijri, A. A., Gyabak, K., Hilligoss, M., Kizilboga, R., & Tomita, K. (2015). Judgment and instructional design: How ID practitioners work in practice. *Performance Improvement Quarterly, 28*(3), 25–49. https://doi.org/10.1002/piq.21198

Gustafson, K. L., & Branch, R. M. (2002). *Survey of instructional development models* (4th ed.). ERIC.

Hansen, B. E. (2010). *Characteristics of context for instructional design* [Doctoral dissertation, Capella University]. ProQuest (Publication Number 041).

Hupe, P., & Hill, M. (2007). Street-Level bureaucracy and public accountability. *Public Administration, 85*(2), 279–299. https://doi.org/10.1111/j.1467-9299.2007.00650.x

Intentional Futures. (2016). *Instructional design in higher education: A report on the role, workflow, and experience of instructional designers.* https://uploads-ssl.webflow.com/61bb092a5c21437cb3a10798/624241a510e63d6f7eee6cd0_Instructional-Design-in-Higher-Education-Report.pdf

Knight, P. T., & Trowler, P. R. (2000). Department-level cultures and the improvement of learning and teaching. *Studies in Higher Education, 25*(1), 69–83. https://doi.org/10.1080/030750700116028

Lowell, V. L., & Ashby, I. V. (2018). Supporting the development of collaboration and feedback skills in instructional designers. *Journal of Computing in Higher Education, 30*(1), 72–92. https://doi.org/10.1007/s12528-018-9170-8

Magnusson, D. (1981). *Situational determinants of stress: An interactional perspective*. University of Stockholm.

Magruder, O., Arnold, D. A., Moore, S., & Edwards, M. (2019). What is an ID? A survey study. *Online Learning*, *23*(3), 137–160. https://doi.org/10.24059/olj.v23i3.1546

McDermott, R., & O'dell, C. (2001). Overcoming cultural barriers to sharing knowledge. *Journal of Knowledge Management*. https://doi.org/10.1108/13673270110384428

Merrill, M. D., Drake, L., Lacy, M. J., Pratt, J., & Group, I. R. (1996). Reclaiming instructional design. *Educational Technology*, *36*(5), 5–7. https://mdavidmerrill.files.wordpress.com/2019/04/reclaiming.pdf

Moore, S. T. (1987). The theory of street-level bureaucracy: A positive critique. *Administration & Society*, *19*(1), 74–94. https://doi.org/10.1177/009539978701900104

Munzenmaier, C. (2014). *Today's instructional designer: Competencies and careers* (Perspectives, Issue). https://www.learningguild.com/insights/178/todays-instructional-designer-competencies-and-careers/

Paais, M., & Pattiruhu, J. R. (2020). Effect of motivation, leadership, and organizational culture on satisfaction and employee performance. *The Journal of Asian Finance, Economics, and Business*, *7*(8), 577–588. https://doi.org/10.13106/jafeb.2020.vol7.no8.577

Reiser, R. A., & Dempsey, J. V. (2012). *Trends and issues in instructional design and technology* (R. A. Reiser & J. V. Dempsey, Eds., 3rd ed.). Pearson.

Richardson, J. C., Ashby, I., Alshammari, A. N., Cheng, Z., Johnson, B. S., Krause, T. S., Lee, D., Randolph, A. E., & Wang, H. (2019). Faculty and instructional designers on building successful collaborative relationships. *Educational Technology Research and Development*, *67*(4), 855–880. https://doi.org/10.1007/s11423-018-9636-4

Schein, E. H. (2010). *Organizational culture and leadership* (Vol. 2). John Wiley & Sons.

Tjosvold, D., & Poon, M. (1998). Dealing with scarce resources: Open-minded interaction for resolving budget conflicts. *Group & Organization Management*, *23*(3), 237–255. https://doi.org/10.1177/1059601198233003

Trekles, A. M. (2011). *University instructional designers: Everyday leadership in the age of accountability*. ERIC. https://files.eric.ed.gov/fulltext/ED543913.pdf

Appendix A
Interview Protocol and Questions

Before we begin, I would like to share a few procedures for our conversation.
With your permission, I would like to video and audio record our session.
Audio/video recording will be done on Zoom.
The digital recording of our conversation will be transcribed.
Pseudonyms for each participant during the transcription process.
The recording and transcription will be kept in a secure location for the duration of, and for, five years after the conclusion of the study.
Although we will be on a first-name basis, no names or identifying comments will be used when I report the results of this session. You can be assured of complete confidentiality.
This interview will last approximately 45–60 minutes.
Have you read and signed the consent form?
Do I have your permission to audio record our interview?
Do you have any questions about it before we begin?

- Could you please share your job position in the department (your job designation/title)?
- How long have you worked in this position?
- What are the functions of this role/position?
- What are the goals of this role/position?
- What, according to you, is the definition of instructional design?
- How did you become an instructional designer?
- Would you describe your educational background (your degree/certifications)?
- Could you describe your day-to-day work in the department?
- What functions do you perform? What are you responsible for?
- How do your current job functions compare with those that are expected of you? (Is there a difference? Could you elaborate?)
- Could you describe the structure/organization of your department?
- How would you describe your working relationships with the faculty and other staff? Can you suggest changes or improvements to courses, systems?

- From your perspective, who should have primary decision-making authority over curricula development and institutional systems? (Could you provide an example? Why do you think so?)
- Think of a project you have designed and completed. Could you walk me through the course development process?
- Whom did you interact with? Could you describe the manner of communication (open door, formal, email, fluid)?
- What resources did you use to do your work? Were they adequate? How?
- What challenges did you face and how did you deal with them?
- What kind of impact or contribution do you think you make to the organization? Could you give some examples (improving curricula, systems, processes)?
- In what ways does the institution and department invest in your professional development (organizing webinars, workshops, registering you for them to ensure you have current knowledge, instructional technology/ LMS training)?
- What strategies do you use to perform all your functions in a satisfactory manner every day?

Index

ADDIE (analysis, design, development, evaluation, implementation of instruction) 8, 49
agent/instructional designer narrative 31; autonomy 32; employee engagement 32–33; flexible decision-making 32; professionalism 32
Anderson, M. C. 14, 21
artificial intelligence (AI) software 11
Ashbaugh, M. L. 14, 19, 20
autonomy 30–33, 71, 74, 75, 77, 81, 83, 92–95, 106
awareness, instructional design 107–108

biases 4, 33–38, 51
Bloom 8
Boling, E. 16

citizen-agent narrative 28–29
client/faculty and learner narrative 33
competencies, instructional design 12, 13, 37
Conditions of Learning 8
confirmability 35–36
constructivism 33
Cope, D. G. 36
coping strategies 70, 76, 77, 92, 94
credibility 35
curriculum development 2, 12, 14, 44

data analysis 45
data collection process 45
deep learning 8
Denzin, N. 113
department cultures 19–20, 71, 78, 87, 93

department structure 70, 77, 85
dependability 35
design functions 54, 57, 61
design methods 59, 65
design process 18, 20, 54, 59, 65
design projects 12, 16, 17, 21, 33
design tasks 53, 61, 62
development functions 61, 102
discretionary flexibility 32
distance education 39, 55, 70
Drysdale, J. 16, 18, 19, 68
dysfunctional cultures 108

education 3, 7, 8, 14, 28, 41, 44
educational technology 50, 52, 54–57, 60–62, 64–67, 98, 102; functions 52, 53, 65
eLearning 1, 7, 9, 14, 41, 43–45, 55, 59, 68
eLearning Guild 9
End College 40, 43–45, 59–65; coping strategies 92; course design 61; educational technology 62; faculty and student liaison 63–64; finite resources 88–89; flexible discretion 90–91; functional fluidity 86–87; informal leadership 64–65; meeting client needs 88; organizational contribution 100–101; personal characteristics 89–90; professional development 91–92; project management 60–61; roles and functions 60; team culture 87–88; team structure and culture 85–86; training 62–63

faculty analysis 61
faculty liaison 51, 52, 55, 58, 63, 66–67, 88
finite resource management 66, 74, 81, 85, 89, 92, 95, 96, 111
flat, team structures 18–19
formal university: definition of instructional design 107
framing factors 30
full-time instructional designers 40, 112
functional fluidity 85–87, 93, 95

Gagne 8
Gardner, J. 15, 21
graphic design 14, 43, 44
Gray, C. M. 16

Hansen, B. E. 16, 17
hierarchical structures 17–19, 31, 66, 67, 77, 93
higher education 1–4, 7–11, 35–38, 40; instructional design in 8–11; sector 3
Hill, M. 106
history 7–11
human learning outcomes 8
human performance technology (HPT) 9
Hupe, P. 106
hybrid system 108–109

informal leaders 51, 52, 64
informal leadership 50–53, 55, 58, 64–67, 76
institutional culture 31, 96, 104, 106, 108, 111
institutional/university narrative 30; ambiguous client expectations 31; finite resources 31; institutional context and culture 30–31
instructional designer job behavior 70, 89, 104, 106, 109–111; institutional culture 104, 106; and organizational culture theory 110–111; personal characteristics 106–107
instructional designers 1–2, 9–11, 14–17, 21, 37, 65, 67, 70, 77, 93–96, 101–102, 109; academic background vs experience 13–14; autonomy 75, 106; availability of resources, influence 20–21;
factors 29, 83, 85, 95; faculty perceptions of 21–22; functions 2, 18, 21, 74, 88, 113; in higher education 2, 35, 38; institutional context and culture, influence 17–20; institutionally defined instructional designer roles 15–17; job roles and functions 66–68; knowledge and skills 11–13; on-the-job behavior 104, 107, 111; perceptions 29, 49–61, 65; perceptions *vs.* official job descriptions 49–68; personal values 14–15; roles and functions 20, 22, 30, 33; street-level divergence 22, 38, 112
instructional design themes 13
instructional technology 1, 7, 39, 40, 43, 44
Intentional Futures 14
internalization 8
interpretivism 33

job functions 32, 65, 102, 110
job goals 29, 30, 98

Lane University 39, 42–43, 54–59, 65, 67, 77–85, 93–95, 99, 101, 104, 109, 111; autonomy/flexible decision-making 83; boxed in 79; department culture 78–79; finite resources 81–82; institutional and department structure 77–78; meeting client needs 80–81; one-way communication 79–80; organizational contribution 99–100; personal characteristics 82–83; professional development 83–85; responsive role 57–59; roles and functions 55; support roles 55–57
leadership 11, 12, 16, 60
learning design 1, 3, 22, 59, 77, 84; systems 1
learning management system (LMS) 10, 11, 15, 17, 18, 20, 21, 37, 40, 44
learning theories 59, 65
Lincoln, Y. 113
Luo, H. 20, 106

macro dimension 29–30
Marshall, C. 45
methodological fluidity 4
micro dimension 29–30
Mitchell, K. 13

narratives 29, 30

one-way communication 79, 80, 82, 83
organizational contribution 15, 29, 30, 45, 98–102, 112; End College 100–101; Lane University 99–100; River University 98–99
organizational culture 110, 112–113
organizational development 2, 30, 34, 37, 98, 99, 101, 104, 110

Park, J.-Y. 20, 106
personal characteristics 74, 75, 77, 82, 83, 89, 90, 92–94, 101, 102, 106, 111, 113
personal values 14–15, 74, 81–83, 89–91, 93–95, 100, 102, 106
personal work ethics 15
Piña, A. A. 20
positionality 36–37
positive communication 64, 85, 87
positive working relations 50, 51, 72, 74, 76, 81, 90, 92–94, 101, 111
positivism 33
professional development 2, 3, 75–77, 83–85, 91, 92, 94, 95, 109; activities 20, 32, 75, 77, 83–85, 91, 95, 109; End College 91–92; Lane University 83–85; River University 75–76
professional growth 76, 84, 85, 91, 109
professional identity 65

qualitative research 4, 33–36

reflexivity 38
relation-building functions 50–52; faculty and student liaison 51; informal leadership 51–52; project management 50–51
relationship-building functions 50, 52, 66, 73, 76, 99
research assumptions 37–38
research design 2–5, 22, 33–34
research process 4, 5, 36, 38
research quality 34–35
research sites 38–39

responsive functions 58, 67, 68, 93, 102, 106
responsive role, Lane University 57–59; faculty and student liaison 58; informal leadership 58–59
Richardson, J. C. 13
River University 39–42, 49–54, 65–67, 70–77, 93–95, 101, 106, 109–111; coping strategies 76–77; culture of autonomy 71–72; department structure 70–71; discrete flexibility/ flexible decision-making 74–75; finite resources 73–74; meeting client needs 72–73; new roles 53–54; organizational contribution 98–99; personal characteristics 74; professional development 75–76; relation-building functions 50–52 (*see also* relation-building functions); roles and functions 50; support functions 52–53 (*see also* supportive/support functions)
Rossman, G. B. 45

sampling criteria 40
Shrock 9
Skinner, B. F. 8
social agency 10
sociological theory 28
state-agent narrative 29
street-level bureaucrats 70–96, 112; End College 85–92; Lane University 77–85; River University 70–77
street-level divergence 28, 29, 31, 34, 77
student liaison 50–53, 55, 58, 60, 63, 66–68, 76, 88
supportive/support functions 16, 50, 52–53, 55, 56, 60, 62–64, 66–67, 74, 88, 102; course design 53; educational technology function 52–53; training 52
support roles 55–57; course design 57; project management 55–56; training 56

Taxonomy of Educational Objectives 8
team hierarchy 91, 93–95
theoretical implications 109–110

theory 28–29
training 12, 14, 32, 50, 52, 53, 55, 56, 60, 62–64, 66, 67, 72
transferability 36
truth value 34

university job descriptions 49, 50, 54, 55, 57, 66, 72, 78
unofficial functions 67, 96, 100

Van Rooij, S. W. 21

working relations 50–52, 62, 66–68, 73, 81–83, 89, 90, 93, 94
workshops 15, 20, 60, 63, 75, 84, 91, 92, 107–109

Yin, R. K. 34

For Product Safety Concerns and Information please contact our EU
representative GPSR@taylorandfrancis.com
Taylor & Francis Verlag GmbH, Kaufingerstraße 24, 80331 München, Germany

www.ingramcontent.com/pod-product-compliance
Lightning Source LLC
Chambersburg PA
CBHW051753230426
43670CB00012B/2271